T0290742

# Finding History Where You Least Expect It

American
Alliance of
Museums

# AMERICAN ALLIANCE OF MUSEUMS

The American Alliance of Museums has been bringing museums together since 1906, helping to develop standards and best practices, gathering and sharing knowledge, and providing advocacy on issues of concern to the entire museum community. Representing more than 35,000 individual museum professionals and volunteers, institutions, and corporate partners serving the museum field, the Alliance stands for the broad scope of the museum community.

The American Alliance of Museums' mission is to champion museums and nurture excellence in partnership with its members and allies.

Books published by AAM further the Alliance's mission to make standards and best practices for the broad museum community widely available.

# Finding History Where You Least Expect It

## Site-Based Strategies for Teaching about the Past

Edited by Jill M. Gradwell
and Kathryn H. Leacock

ROWMAN & LITTLEFIELD
*Lanham • Boulder • New York • London*

Published by Rowman & Littlefield
An imprint of The Rowman & Littlefield Publishing Group, Inc.
4501 Forbes Boulevard, Suite 200, Lanham, Maryland 20706
www.rowman.com

6 Tinworth Street, London SE11 5AL, United Kingdom

British Library Cataloguing in Publication Information Available

**Library of Congress Cataloging-in-Publication Data Available**

Library of Congress Control Number: 2020934264
ISBN 978-1-5381-4087-1 (cloth : alk. paper)
ISBN 978-1-5381-4088-8 (pbk. alk. paper)
ISBN 978-1-5381-4089-5 (electronic)

♾™ The paper used in this publication meets the minimum requirements of
American National Standard for Information Sciences—Permanence of Paper
for Printed Library Materials, ANSI/NISO Z39.48-1992.

# Contents

# Preface

Generally speaking, if you work in a museum, you love museums. Accordingly, to write a book for the museum profession is akin to preaching to the choir. As a profession, we pride ourselves on our resourcefulness, collegiality, and willingness to share what works (and offer guidance on what doesn't). For almost a decade, we were the recipients of several federal grants through the Department of Education and the National Endowment for the Humanities and led numerous professional development workshops for teachers that focused on teaching history using museums and landmarks. While the topics, cohorts, and focus differed slightly, the overarching goal of providing teachers with the necessary tools, comfort level, and awareness of how to use cultural sites in their classroom was pervasive. Consequently, we saw a whole host of museums, cultural organizations, and museum professionals pull together to provide workshops, offer professional development opportunities, and share their respective institution with the various teacher cohorts. Many of these programs were new and innovative, and they provided historical content when the teachers were not expecting it.

At one of our workshops, we could feel the tension and confusion in the room when a group of social studies teachers gathered around a table at a science museum. While they didn't say it aloud, we sensed they were wondering, "Why are we here?" So sparked the idea for this book; how can we share the great projects that were born out of these endeavors (and more) with a wider audience? The edited volume, *Finding History Where You Least Expect It: Site-Based Strategies for Teaching about the Past*, explores creative and engaging museum programs across varied sites. The chapters highlight how museum programming, object-based learning, and site-specific education can impact learning for people of all ages. The goal is to appeal to museum educators, curriculum developers, university students, and teachers to illustrate the variety of programming you can do in your own backyard.

The following eighteen chapters have been brought together to illustrate how history can be taught (and learned) in the most unlikely places or in the most unlikely ways. Museums and cultural institutions are striving to remain relevant in an ever-changing landscape. This volume looks at organizations that have challenged the traditional offerings expected of their organization and are working to break into new markets and develop new programs for diverse and previously untapped audiences.

Western New York and the City of Buffalo have oftentimes been described as the "City of Good Neighbors." As a population, we are a close-knit community and inherently proud, even in the unwavering support of our sports teams. The same can be said for many American cities and small towns. We wanted to take this opportunity to share all the great things that are happening at upstate New York's cultural institutions that can be reproduced elsewhere. While the featured institutions are regionally linked, the ideas in *Finding History Where You Least Expect It* can be replicated in organizations anywhere. While we advocate for site-based programs, the authors also offer suggestions for replicating their ideas in school classrooms or with minimal financial investment. Most programs can be scaled accordingly and are open to further modifications.

A review of the recent publications in the field of museum education and the teaching of history shows a need for a book that looks at learning through the lens of the program itself. While publications exist that explore educational pedagogy and programming according to museum type, this volume explores history through the lens of the specific program. The authors walk the reader through their ideas, development, implementation, and successes, allowing others the ability to learn from their endeavor in order to build a unique program for themselves. The chapters are written by those most closely associated with the program, providing insider guidance through every aspect of its development. Let their drive to try something new be the catalyst for your organization. Use their experience to persuade your board of managers, executive director, or superintendent that there is always something new that can be tried and achieved.

The goal of this book is to further encourage teachers, museum professionals, and emerging museum professionals to think outside the box. Don't be encumbered by the outdated definition of your historic site or stuck taking your students on the same field trip because that is always where they go in fourth grade. As a field, museum professionals are always looking for new and inventive ways to share their passion, collection, and content. It shouldn't be confined to a formal field trip.

The Niagara Falls Underground Railroad Heritage Center had the opportunity to start from the beginning, building their exhibits, interpretation themes, and programs from scratch. Outlined here is the public program *Freedom Conversations*, which builds on the work of the International Coalition of Sites of Conscience to deliver a sensitive historical topic to a contemporary audience. The Buffalo Museum of Science built on a collection that had remained underutilized since the turn of the twentieth century, illustrating that material can always be reconfigured, reworked, and reinterpreted to become another program for a new audience. The staff of the Theodore Roosevelt Inaugural National Historic Site thought about the activities that the original inhabitants of their historic house would do for entertainment and replicated an evening of gaming for a millennial audience.

Singing in a cemetery? Learning from gingerbread? Board games and beer in a historic house? These are just a few of the questions that are answered in this volume. We love what we do, and we want that passion for learning to be contagious—with the right program, even the most stubborn patron can learn when they are not expecting to. Let this collection of chapters inspire you to create the next big program, a call to action, history where you least expect it!

# Acknowledgments

The very nature of this project is collaborative, and we found ourselves over-whelmed with the outpouring of support for the initial idea. We have always been fortunate to work with such an amazing group of museum groupies, and we hope that this volume shows what a close-knit group we are. We are extremely grateful to those who contributed to this volume and to those who granted permission for us to use their ideas and photographs, and offered feedback on the chapters while in progress.

We are also thankful to those organizations that wanted to participate but were already overcommitted and overwhelmed with their current roles and responsibilities that one more thing on their plate would cause it to tip completely. We understand.

We want to acknowledge the support from our own organizations, Marisa Wigglesworth, President and CEO of the Buffalo Museum of Science, who supported this project from the beginning. Also, the State University of New York Buffalo State College for the sabbatical release time and the financial support endowed by the late Edward O. "E. O." Smith Jr., former Chair of the Department of History and Social Studies Education.

Our executive editor, Charles Harmon, whose enthusiastic and timely response to our initial proposal gave us the boost we needed to continue with this work. His unwavering encouragement and lightning-fast email responses were sincerely appreciated. We thank Charles, Erinn Slanina, and the rest of their colleagues at Rowman & Littlefield for their guidance and support in publishing this volume.

We are ever so grateful to our immediate and extended families who supported us along the way. And finally, most of all, we want to thank our children, Camden, Kellen, Declan, Elias, and Evelyn, who help us to continue to view museums and cultural sites with fresh perspectives and find history where even we least expect it.

## Chapter One

# Freedom Conversations

## *Connecting Past to Present with Facilitated Dialogue*

### Christine Bacon

Located on the international border with Canada, the Niagara Falls Underground Railroad Heritage Center is an innovative, experiential history museum. Our mission is "to reveal authentic stories of Underground Railroad freedom seekers and abolitionists in Niagara Falls, that inspire visitors to recognize modern injustices that stem from slavery and take action toward an equitable society."[1] The heritage center was designed and constructed to align with the principles of the International Coalition of Sites of Conscience, self-described as "the only global network of historic sites, museums and memory initiatives that connect past struggles to today's movements for human rights."[2] The permanent exhibition, *One More River to Cross*, consists of four galleries that use scenic buildouts, animated original artwork, interactive media, and artifacts to immerse visitors in antebellum Niagara Falls. Here, they explore the crucial role its location, geography, and courageous residents—particularly its African American residents—played in the Underground Railroad. Large wall-mounted quotations throughout the historic galleries and the final fifth gallery, called the Freedom Gallery, encourage visitors to connect this history to their own lives. The exhibit *One More River to Cross* at the Niagara Falls Underground Railroad Heritage Center was selected as a 2019 Award of Excellence winner by the Leadership in History awards committee of the American Association for State and Local History, the nation's most prestigious competition for recognition of achievement in state and local history.

When it opened in May 2018, the Niagara Falls Underground Railroad Heritage Center was the first new cultural attraction in the City of Niagara Falls, New York, in more than thirty-five years. Much anticipation surrounded the opening, and from the very start, we knew we wanted to exceed expectations and to be at the forefront of Underground Railroad interpretation. To that end,

1

**Figure 1.1. The US Custom House in Niagara Falls was transformed into the Niagara Falls Underground Railroad Heritage Center.**
Courtesy of the Niagara Falls Underground Railroad Heritage Center.

we designed the permanent exhibit to enhance what we knew would become our signature public program: *Freedom Conversations*. In the year since we opened, our facilitated dialogue program *Freedom Conversations* has indeed hit the mark. Not only is this sixty-minute guided tour program run daily for walk-in guests, but organizations also collaborate with us to use the program in innovative ways. The *Freedom Conversations* program has become of, by, and for our community in ways that exceed even our own expectations.

While guided tours are the signature staple of history museums, traditional lecture-style tours have minimal impact because learning is passive, and, therefore, content retention is minimal. We asked how this new heritage center could do more than merely provide historical content to visitors. Building on the canon of traditional historical interpretation, *Freedom Conversations* focuses on facilitated dialogue. Because the content of each tour depends on the involvement of the visitors, no two tours are ever the same. When visitors are actively engaged in creating meaning from the historical content, the result is a powerful, impactful learning experience.

*Freedom Conversations* is the means by which the heritage center makes the history of the Underground Railroad relevant for visitors today. The program helps us achieve our mission. We admittedly have a social justice goal. Our vision is to encourage visitors to take action for civil and human rights and to create global change that begins in the Niagara Falls community.

Niagara Falls played a unique role in the Underground Railroad. Because it sits on an international border, freedom seekers arriving here were mere steps away from liberty, after having endured perilous travel for hundreds of miles. Recognizing this, interpretation at the heritage center focuses on the strength and agency of the individuals who used the Underground Railroad network to claim their own freedom. Freedom seekers themselves are at the heart of our stories. The heritage center's approach to Underground Railroad interpretation is not to ask how communities of African descent *survived,* but rather to demonstrate how these communities *thrived.* In alignment with this philosophical approach, in our narratives freedom seekers are not beleaguered victims of an oppressive system; they are triumphant heroes of subterfuge and resistance. The *Freedom Conversations* interpretive approach is to communicate stories demonstrating that on the shores of the Niagara River, freedom seekers stood as powerful masters of their own destiny, just as many people today take great risks to control their own fate.

While the Underground Railroad must be set within the broader context of the institutionalized system of chattel slavery that once existed in the United States, slavery, per se, is not one of the heritage center's primary interpretive themes. Rather, we focus on the inspirational network of people of African descent who lived in, worked in, or passed through Niagara Falls in pursuit of freedom. Moreover, the *Freedom Conversations* program connects their stories to the continued struggle for all people to live free from oppression. The primary interpretive themes for the program are as follows: (1) the Underground Railroad in Niagara Falls: in Niagara Falls, the Underground Railroad operated as an overt resistance to slavery, led by people of African descent, and the dramatic landscape of Niagara Falls drew tourists from the southern United States, which, when coupled with its geographic location on the shore of the Niagara River—a narrow crossing point along the lengthy Great Lakes water border between the United States and Canada—made Niagara Falls one of the most significant crossing points for freedom seekers on the Underground Railroad; (2) freedom: the right to live freely is a universal human desire to which all visitors can relate; and (3) social justice: historical stories of resistance to oppression provide insight into current struggles for freedom and can motivate individuals to work toward a just and equitable society.

*Freedom Conversations* at the heritage center has several overarching goals: provide documented, historically accurate information about the people and events that define the unique role Niagara Falls played in the Underground Railroad as a border crossing between the United States and Canada; promote active narratives that give agency to the authentic, yet little-known individuals of African descent who lived in, worked in, or passed through Niagara Falls in search of liberty; help visitors recognize that some modern injustices have direct roots in slavery, while other contemporary struggles parallel those of eighteenth- and nineteenth-century freedom seekers; and motivate visitors to work toward a more just and equitable society.

Due to the heritage center's location in the urban core of an international tourist destination, the audience for *Freedom Conversations* is diverse. Our target audience is the local community within the City of Niagara Falls, with a special focus on residents of African descent. The City of Niagara Falls has suffered both a population and an economic decline over the past half-decade. The population has dropped from more than 100,000 residents in the 1950s to less than 50,000 as of 2018. Although 87.7 percent of the population has at least a high school diploma, only 17 percent have earned a bachelor's degree or higher. A significant portion of residents live below the poverty level, with rates as high as 64.8 percent in the most economically disadvantaged census tract, which is located near the heritage center.[3] Reminding residents of their city's inspiring history provides a sense of pride to a community that has not felt it had much to celebrate in recent decades.

Our secondary audience consists of the wider western New York community. Outside the urban cores of Niagara Falls and Buffalo, the population is ethnically homogenous, with most residents being of European descent. Economic indicators are higher in several suburbs, but in small towns and rural areas, economic hardships prevail, as the entire area (including the City of Niagara Falls) was impacted by the withdrawal of automotive, steel, and other manufacturing industries in the last decades of the twentieth century.

A third audience consists of out-of-town tourists who visit Niagara Falls each year. Estimates as to the size of this audience vary, but generally number in the millions annually. This audience is widely diverse and cannot easily be categorized into any particular homogenous group. Drawn to Niagara Falls to witness the natural wonder of the falls themselves, visitors hail from across the world with vastly different socioeconomic, educational, and linguistic backgrounds.

Recognizing this diversity, the team at the heritage center nevertheless determined to find common ground. We settled upon the notion of "freedom." The quest for liberty, or self-determination, is one to which all visitors can relate in ways that are uniquely personal to the individual. All of us have felt bound or constrained in one way or another, whether by authority figures, by lack of economic resources, or by other limiting factors. Likewise, we have all sought to free ourselves from the limitations that hold us back, whether in our personal or professional lives. This desire to control one's own life is a universal theme, and the *Freedom Conversations* program is designed to meet visitors wherever they are on their personal journey to freedom.

To do this, *Freedom Conversations* relies heavily on the facilitated dialogue historical interpretation technique.[4] Facilitated dialogue tours use a strategically designed set of questions—an arc of dialogue—to guide participants into a structured, meaningful conversation about a challenging or controversial topic. Through constructive sharing and listening, facilitated dialogue provides a venue in which proactive citizenship skills can be modeled, learned, and practiced. Specifically, the *Freedom Conversations* program at the heritage center aligns with the facilitated dialogue techniques taught by the International Coalition of Sites of Conscience, whose mission is to connect the past to modern social justice issues—"to turn memory to action."[5] *Freedom Conversations* takes place at the heritage center daily for walk-in visitors and is offered to groups upon request. The program takes approximately sixty minutes and encompasses the entire museum.

Tours begin just outside the heritage center in a public atrium where one wall provides a visual general overview of the Underground Railroad. Here, facilitators begin a conversation with visitors, getting everyone to say something (anything), setting ground rules that include listening to one another with mutual respect, and soliciting an affirmative agreement from every participant that they will honor the process, the history, and one another. These initial steps are crucial to the success of the program. If visitors actively voice an answer to even one introductory question such as, "Where are you from?" they will be more likely to speak a second time in response to a more challenging question. Likewise, if everyone has affirmatively acknowledged an agreement to speak and listen with respect, the discussion is more likely to remain civil.

Once inside the heritage center, facilitators weave hyper-local historical content with questions for the tour participants to answer. Nearly all of the

**Figure 1.2.  Visitors engaged in *Freedom Conversations* in the center's exhibition space.**
Courtesy of the Niagara Falls Underground Railroad Heritage Center.

history presented inside the museum focuses exclusively on people and events in Niagara Falls. Questions are of four types and follow an "arc of dialogue." Facilitators begin with phase one questions, which are designed to build community, are non-threatening, and are relatively easy to answer. Phase two questions invite visitors to think about and share their own experiences. Phase three questions challenge visitors to "dig deeper into their assumptions and to probe underlying social conditions that inform our diversity of perspectives."[6] Finally, phase four questions provide closure to the experience by reinforcing a sense of community. Visitors may be asked to reflect on what they heard or what they want to know more about. Not all tours will flow through the entire narrative arc from phase one to phase four. Some tours will cycle through this arc several times on multiple different topics. It all depends on the visitors.

The program's success is not due solely to the adoption of one interpretive technique. Before we launched the first *Freedom Conversations*, there were many months of preparation involving a conscious shift in the traditional systemic structures that typify many museum interpretive programs. Ultimately, our approach is to model the change in perspective in the very infrastructure of our organization—both in terms of human capital and built resources. The *Freedom Conversations* program is more than a one-off program for us; it is the outward manifestation of an internal commitment to take action for civil and human rights and create global change that begins in the Niagara Falls community. Facilitated dialogue is our primary tool in realizing this vision, both internally with our own staff and externally with our visitors.

With a brand-new museum to create from the ground up, we had a unique opportunity to build facilitated dialogue directly into the permanent exhibits, which would then be used to enhance our *Freedom Conversations.* This commitment to facilitated dialogue programming was first memorialized in the request for proposals (RFP) seeking a design firm to create the permanent exhibition at the heritage center. Specifically, in the "Design and Goals" section of the RFP, the expectation was for the design to align with the worldwide movement of the International Coalition of Sites of Conscience. Their mission states, "We are sites, individuals, and initiatives activating the power of places of memory to engage the public in connecting past and present in order to envision and shape a more just and humane future."[7]

The contracted design firm built on the work of the International Coalition of Sites of Conscience to design the permanent galleries. Although the *Freedom Conversations* program makes use of the entire exhibit, it relies heavily on the "Freedom Gallery" and its "Freedom Videos," both of which incorporated the International Coalition of Sites of Conscience into the design process, with the Coalition's Braden Paynter participating as a consultant. When it came time to train our historical interpreters for the *Freedom Conversations* program, we again brought in Paynter to lead the facilitated dialogue portion of the training.

Before we could train the staff, we had to hire them. Here, too, we tried hard to "walk the walk" rather than simply "talk the talk." For far too long, the narrative of the Underground Railroad has been told from the perspective of the white abolitionist, aside from Harriet Tubman. The predominant narrative generally ignores the brave black men, women, and children who operated the network of people and places by which enslaved individuals *freed themselves*. Although white abolitionists helped, the Underground Railroad was primarily driven by people who were held in bondage against their will. As such, who should rightly control the historical narrative of the Underground Railroad? From whose perspective should the story be told? Whose voice should guide the conversation about chattel slavery's impact on twenty-first-century society?

Here it is necessary to confront a disappointing reality in the museum profession: its profound lack of diversity. A 2015 study by the Mellon Foundation documented that 84 percent of curators, conservators, educators, and leadership in art museums are white non-Hispanic.[8] Those of us on the ground in history museums know our statistics are similar. In 1992, the American Alliance of Museums (AAM) published *Excellence and Equity: Education and the Public Dimension of Museums*.[9] In it, AAM's task force advised that to stay relevant and to carry out an educational mission, museums must reflect the diversity of our society "in all activities and at all levels."[10] The task force recommended widening the arena for recruitment of professional staff members. This is further supported by the new AAM 2019 publication *Diversity, Equity, Accessibility, and Inclusion in Museums*.[11]

The heritage center does this in several ways. One method has been to actively recruit historical interpreters for *Freedom Conversations* at a grassroots level in communities of color. A second method has been to value an applicant's passion for the work and our mission at least as highly as we value a background in museum studies or public history. A third method is that we have eschewed the long-standing reliance on volunteer docents in favor of a fully paid interpretive staff. Reliance upon the people who can afford to forgo income by volunteering can lead to a homogenous frontline staff in terms of both ethnic background and age. Making the financial commitment to find, train, and pay a museum staff drawn from a nontraditional museum applicant pool has presented challenges, but the rewards are far greater.

The feedback from visitors to our interpretive approach has been overwhelmingly positive. Visitors have described the experience as "profoundly moving" and as having "brought [them] to tears more than once." Community stakeholders have sought out the *Freedom Conversations* program to

**Figure 1.3. Learning the stories of others is a key component to *Freedom Conversations.***
Courtesy of the Niagara Falls Underground Railroad Heritage Center.

help spark dialogue between groups that do not always see eye to eye. For example, *Freedom Conversations* helped members of a predominately black church in Niagara Falls find common ground with leaders from a Jewish organization in Buffalo. Similarly, we were approached by regional management of a national retailer to provide a *Freedom Conversations* program for the company's mostly white managers, with the goal of helping them to better understand the perspectives of their frontline staff, most of whom are people of color.

When done well, *Freedom Conversations* is applied history at its finest. Grounded in academic research conducted by Judith Wellman, PhD, the program connects historical people and events with present-day issues that impact the lives of participants on the tour. For example, conversations about abolitionists who defied the Fugitive Slave Act blend with questions about whether and under what circumstances breaking the law is justified today. The conversation might lead to a discussion about how laws are created in the first place, and by whom. The facilitated dialogue narrative arc of questions might conclude with a conversation about civic engagement, voting rights, and the steps visitors can take to influence legislative agendas at the local, state, and national levels. Or program participants might lead the conversation to a discussion about the worldwide refugee crisis, the rise of neo-Nazism in the twenty-first century, the absence of an Equal Rights Amendment to the US Constitution, the for-profit prison system, or any of a thousand other threads that tie one movement for civil rights to another. All of these conversations are rooted in the heritage center's stories of the Underground Railroad in Niagara Falls.

The essence of the Underground Railroad was resistance to oppression and an unyielding quest for personal liberty. So long as oppression remains in any form, the spirit of the Underground Railroad will continue to inspire freedom seekers. We foresee the *Freedom Conversations* program remaining relevant for a long time to come.

## NOTES

1. Niagara Falls Underground Railroad Heritage Center, *Brand Document*, adopted March 2018.

2. International Coalition of Sites of Conscience, accessed July 10, 2019, https://www.sitesofconscience.org/en/home/.

3. "Quick Facts: Niagara Falls City, New York," United States Census Bureau, accessed February 11, 2020, https://www.census.gov/quickfacts/niagarafalls citynewyork.

4. "Facilitated Dialogue," International Coalition of Sites of Conscience, accessed July 10, 2019, https://www.sitesofconscience.org/wp-content/uploads/2019/01/Dialogue -Overview.pdf.

5. "Facilitated Dialogue."

6. "Facilitated Dialogue."

7. "Membership Application," International Coalition of Sites of Conscience, accessed February 17, 2020, https://www.sitesofconscience.org/wp-content/up loads/2016/06/membership_application_2016.pdf.

8. Roger Schonfeld and Mariet Westermann, *Art Museum Staff Demographic Survey* (The Andrew W. Mellon Foundation, 2015), 9.

9. American Alliance of Museums, *Excellence and Equity: Education and the Public Dimension of Museums* (Washington, DC: 1992).

10. American Alliance of Museums, *Excellence and Equity*, 16.

11. Johnnetta Betsch Cole and Laura L. Lott, eds., *Diversity, Equity, Accessibility, and Inclusion in Museums* (New York: Rowman & Littlefield, 2019).

## Chapter Two

# "The Most Boring Thing in the World"

## Scrapbooks and the Archives

### Daniel DiLandro

One might expect to find history in an archive. Why, then, is an archival program included in a volume claiming to illuminate where unexpected historical learning can occur? Archives are, by definition, a place where records, documents, and historical materials are preserved and housed: another form of collecting institution. While we expect a museum to have a sizable annual visitation, do we expect the same from an archive? Just as other cultural organizations deal with the notion of relevancy, so, too, does an archival repository. What types of programming can an archive produce? Certainly, we can expect content-based lectures; what would be unexpected? As an archivist at the E. H. Butler Library on the State University of New York Buffalo State College's campus in Buffalo, New York, my goal is to illustrate how the written word can be used to foster dialogue, not only through the historical narrative, but through a discussion about the role of the source at the time of production and today.

As an archivist, I am lucky to have access to sometimes "unexpected" primary source material that I can introduce at public programs and incorporate into my teaching. Archival material provides certain perspectives that may differ from secondary source material that sometimes presents biased, incomplete, or factually incorrect solutions. Take, for instance, the Thomas Penney Leon Czolgosz Trial Scrapbooks (Penney Scrapbooks). This archival material can inform the public on not only general history topics and the assassination of President William McKinley at Buffalo's Pan-American Exposition in 1901, but also disciplines such as law, the nature of early twentieth-century newspaper reporting, the role and treatment of marginalized populations, and other areas of study. I did not fully explain the intellectual depth of this material as I was discussing the content of the scrapbooks during one of my public presentations to a college student. Merely focusing on a litany of newspaper

**Figure 2.1.   Three of the scrapbook volumes. Their plain covers say little about the wealth of content within.**
Courtesy of the Buffalo History Museum Library and Archives, Mss. D2011-01, Leon Czolgosz trial scrapbooks.

clippings that described the events around the shooting of the president led that student to perhaps correctly exclaim, "Well, that sounds like the most boring thing in the world!" Was the student's comment accurate? Or was the angle of the presentation to blame for her premature conclusion? Challenge accepted.

Since then, I have modified my explanation of the material in my public presentations to include how this collection of articles provides a wealth of understanding about the culture of the time, and how the avenues of research are not limited to a single presidential assassination. Notably, these Penney Scrapbooks necessarily describe a specific research topic, but most scrapbooks or collections of this type will provide a similarly "unexpected" foray into historical research and other potential areas of interest.

But how are these scrapbooks unique unto themselves, and how are they similar in content and teaching material to any other scrapbook? What the Penney Scrapbooks describe is a record of then–Erie County District Attorney Thomas Penney's newspaper clippings related to the 1901 assassination of President William McKinley by anarchist Leon Czolgosz at the Pan-American Exposition in Buffalo, New York. Colloquially, local individuals refer to these as the "Pan-Am scrapbooks," but this is not really correct. What these clippings are *not* is the history of the "Pan-Am" itself, but, in effect, research material for District Attorney Penney in his development of a court case against Leon Czolgosz, the assassin of President McKinley. I made this mistake in describing the material to my "bored" audience member—but now I am aware to be much more specific in describing the contents of the material.

The Penney Scrapbooks themselves are housed in the Research Library at the Buffalo History Museum and are available for research. The Buffalo History Museum was founded by the Buffalo Historical Society in 1862. Its early collection contained regional paintings, photographs, artifacts, and manuscripts. By the turn of the twentieth century, a larger space was needed for its burgeoning collection, and an opportunity presented itself during the planning of the World's Fair, the 1901 Pan-American Exposition. The New York State Building, designed by Buffalo architect George Cary, would become the museum's new home after the close of the fair. Today, the Buffalo History Museum's collection contains more than 100,000 physical objects, over 200,000 photographs, and 20,000 books reflecting western New York's story. The museum's Research Library is an archival center responsible for all two-dimensional items in its collection: books, pamphlets, letters, diaries, personal papers, organizational and business records, periodicals, newspapers, photographs, postcards, prints, drawings, posters, maps, atlases, microfilms, DVDs, and scrapbooks.

The Penney Scrapbooks focus on mostly local newspaper articles from various sources that describe events surrounding the assassination of President McKinley; the life of the assassin, Leon Czolgosz; evaluations of possible co-conspirators, such as anarchist Emma Goldman; and quotes from others somehow associated with the crime, for instance some interviews of the hotel proprietor where Czolgosz lodged locally. Through digital replication, I have used examples of both the articles themselves as well as the particular layout, that is, the original order in which Penney (or his secretary) fixed the articles into place.

The most comprehensive description of the scrapbooks is the OCLC/WorldCat catalog record for the material, which reads, in part: "Leon Czolgosz trial scrapbooks, 1901-1911. . . . This collection consists of three scrapbooks of newspaper clippings compiled by Thomas Penney during the trial of Leon Czolgosz. Most of the third scrapbook consists of blank pages."[1] Included in this record is the notation that the author/creator was "Thomas Penney," and the primary subject headings are: "Czolgosz, Leon F., -- 1873?-1901. Goldman, Emma, -- 1869-1940. McKinley, William, -- 1843-1901." Further general subjects (such as "Anarchists -- United States -- History," "Presidents -- Assassination -- United States," "Scrapbooks," et al.) round out the access points in that catalog record, and it describes the material well.

Many primary and secondary sources can explain the history of the Pan-American Exposition much more fully for researchers. The Penney Scrapbooks are not really one of these. While the hundreds of newspaper clippings included here do often naturally speak of the exposition insofar as it was "the scene of the crime," to refer scholars of that event to this resource is akin to providing a single unsourced Internet web page as a citation. The trial clippings are essential as the prosecutor's research material; they are, simply, not a comprehensive resource to learn about the Pan-American Exposition.

But knowing that these clippings were placed and pasted by "Mr. Penney" (as he is constantly referred to in print) or an associate under his watch is, so to speak, to get into his mind. Archival science teaches the principle of original order. It is sometimes impossible for archivists to re-create this, say, when masses of personal papers are delivered with no discernable arrangement, or notably, when the order is made incoherent. When original order is maintained, it is possible for a researcher to re-create the mindset of the creator—in this case, Mr. Penney—and to provide essential springboards into other areas of research. Let's examine some clear, specific threads of inquiry that, notable by their consistent presence, must have been of interest to Mr. Penney and that can surely inspire student scholars and researchers.

For instance, what should researchers make of Mr. Penney having placed two *Buffalo Enquirer* articles together, one headlined "Eager to Lynch the Assassin" and the other "Crowds Were Not Vicious." (The latter article includes the rather "unexpected" line: "The people simply wanted to learn what they could.") We could be tempted to imagine that Penney is playing with us, highlighting the absurdity of some (much?) of the reporting, which, as we shall investigate, is usually rather specious. But we must remember the use of the scrapbooks, which is the district attorney's own reference material. Therefore, it is much more likely that Penney placed these at-odds headlines together to remind himself of the polarized civic temperament as he proceeded to and prepared for the Czolgosz trial.

Again, contradictory reporting, "fake news" so to speak, is endemic to any larger collections of newspaper articles from various sources, so the larger themes discussed here can be replicated from any similar source material.

Extant trial transcripts show District Attorney Penney asking defendant Czolgosz routine questions, such as the latter's place of residence upon his arrival to Buffalo, which was "[a]t Nowak's."[2] Ancillary reporting from the newspaper articles as well as verification from Buffalo city directories indicate that John Nowak was a hotel proprietor on Broadway Avenue, and it would make sense that Penney included references to "Nowak's" in his reference clippings in order to open this line of questioning during the trial. The verification with outside sources underscores the essentiality of authentication of data with supporting documentation and resources.

But even the "Nowak clippings" provide immensely valuable gateways into other areas of scholarship. For example, Nowak, "indignant" at being

**Figure 2.2.   Page showing the headline "Czolgosz Guilty and Must Die in Electric Chair!" as pasted in one of the Penney Scrapbooks.**
Courtesy of the Buffalo History Museum Library and Archives, Mss. D2011-01, Leon Czolgosz trial scrapbooks.

questioned by authorities after the shooting, is quoted as saying that Czolgosz had gone for a shave on the morning of the assassination. "Did they arrest the razor? . . . He bought a bag of peanuts up the street of [*sic*] an Italian. Why don't they arrest the peanut man?" I regard this quote as being too good to be true, more than likely a journalistic invention. Just as the fixed clippings provide internal context for one another, we must consider the context of the assassination of President McKinley in terms of larger history.

"Our" John Nowak does not appear in the 1900 Federal or 1905 New York State census, at least at the Broadway address (though twenty-two men of that name appear in these sources, if living elsewhere), so it is impossible to know his age. Still, the 1901 murder of the president was a mere thirty-six years after the assassination of President Lincoln, and only twenty years after that of President Garfield. Can we assume that Nowak lived through, or was at least aware, of those fraught events? And, if so, he may have known of the terrible fate of proprietor Mary Surratt, who housed Lincoln's killers, paying with her life for that. So, should we assume that Nowak's putative (but perfect and perfectly glib) quote is more of a journalistic invention?

The inclusion of other individuals and their alleged quotations in the Penney Scrapbooks have darker connotations, though they are sometimes similarly impossible to verify. For example, anarchist Emma Goldman, whom Czolgosz cited as an inspiration for the assassination, but who was also exonerated from direct involvement. She is the subject of a large-fonted clipping in the scrapbooks: "'Bombs! Bombs! Bombs! Streams of Blood,' Says Emma Goldman. Frenzied Woman Gives This Recipe for the Cure of Social Inequalities."

Did Goldman actually say this? Available resources cannot verify this quote. Perhaps Goldman thought this, and she may have easily agreed to the concept in spirit, but it is impossible to affirm this line. As with so many other clippings, though, there is no byline and no real supporting evidence (specific dates of this interview, for example) that would warrant the truth of this statement. I point out these lax standards (and frequent inventions) by writers in the era of so-called "yellow journalism" and ask how this is different from contemporary Internet clickbait? It is all created to sell newspapers, to sell web advertising. And who would not spend a few cents to read a (purported) rather lunatic interview with a "frenzied" female anarchist?

Along these lines, there is the curious case of Peter Thomas. Toward the end of the series of clippings, one local article—dated November 5, 1901, long after the Pan-American Exposition, the assassination, and even the execution of Czolgosz—is headlined "Nearly a Riot at a Funeral." This article describes an attack at a "prominent Italian's funeral." But *why* was this article included in the Penney Scrapbooks, clearly placed with (if at the end) of the Pan-American Exposition and Czolgosz series of clippings? Barring the discovery of Penney's journal or other material created by him that could explain his thought process, we must employ suppositions. That the individual was called Peter Thomas, not Pietro Tomaselli or something like, is already curious. Was Penney suspecting that he may have to become personally involved given his professional role as the district attorney? Is there something deeper, some relationship Peter Thomas had to Czolgosz and a presidential assassination?

Researchers may see a correlation. Though not included in Penney's local newspaper clippings, we can discover that some non-regional newspaper outlets, reporting perhaps twelve hours after the shooting, tell of the assassin, "Leon Czolgosso, a Pole."[3] Nightmarish linguistic chimeras aside, even this one incorrect spelling may set researchers upon a fascinating path. As always, we ask, "Why?" Why was the name misreported? Was this simply a mistake in transmitting the surely rushed bulletin? Or is there more at play here? Can it relate to Mr. Penney's inclusion of the "Italian funeral" clipping?

As with any large numbers of new immigrant populations, Poles and Italians were, as evidenced in the Penney articles, looked at with—to put it kindly—"askance," generally noted as being somewhat criminal, if not completely human. Italian anarchists had assassinated that nation's king the year prior to the McKinley killing. Is it safe to assume that Penney had this in mind when literally pasting the Peter Thomas article into his reference scrapbook? And is it logical to posit that the *Boston Daily Globe* was at least biased toward assuming that the assassin might be Italian, hence the addition of the final "o" to his name? Was this a prelude to 1920's farcical Sacco and Vanzetti trial? While specific to the Penney Scrapbooks, errors of this type are frequent in all newspaper clipping collections.

In any case, the editor of the local *Arbeiter-Zeitung* (the local German "Workers' Newspaper") was quick to distance his politics as well as the German community from the shooting; and this notice, along with details about commendable pity from Britain and Germany (both "established" populations in the Buffalo metro area at the time), is significantly included in Penney's clippings. Without time travel and telepathy, we cannot be certain why. But other articles in Penney's admittedly artificial collection bolster the supposition regarding potential race-relation fears. One article hints darkly that the assassination was "Ordered from Rome," and it and other articles emphasize Czolgosz's parents' Roman Catholic faith.

Other marginalized groups do not fare terribly well either. James Benjamin "Big Jim" Parker, an African American and widely hailed hero, who tackled Czolgosz after the latter fired shots at the president, is quoted in dialect: "If it weren't fo' me that murderer would of fiahed dem three shot fum his pistol." Is this an accurate, verbatim account of Parker's words? Is it even true?

However, President McKinley's actions are detailed, often contradictorily depending on the source (and its political bent) and the date it was published, in what can only be described as heroic and religious terms. A mere selection of the many alleged details of the president's death include the following: "McKinley died the death of a soldier, like a man"; "The President, when first shot, felt only pity"; and on and on in this vein.

Ida McKinley, the president's wife, is often referred to after the shooting, but she is never quoted, generally being described as in the throes of "nervous collapse." This is understandable, but such reporting might prove interesting for the researcher who may find useful social parallels in terms of providing "a voice" or "agency" to individuals directly involved in an incident.

Though there are several different versions of his final words, several outlets insist that McKinley quoted the song "Nearer, My God, to Thee," the most fantastic reading as follows: "Nearer, my God, to Thee . . . tho' it be a cross . . . His will be – done; – not – ours." And *finis*! Again, where Czolgosz is portrayed as becoming more and more bestial in prison, where the Eastern European anarchist Emma Goldman is "frenzied," we might be suspicious of the president's final reported words and bearing.

Again, though, is it possible to conclusively refute this reporting? As more and more resources are made publicly and digitally available, it is possible for them to compare and contrast various accounts; but all of us may be unable to categorically "prove" the sometimes obvious "fake news" that was published. The ancient Greeks had a goddess of rumor, as described by Homer in the *Iliad*. "Fake news" is nothing new; and, at least in some cases here, it seems that sources merely quoted one another and did not have reporters present to describe their own firsthand accounts.

Sometimes, though, we can damage, if not challenge, facts that are reported as truth. Clippings reveal that "[t]he blow," that is, the president's death eight days after the shooting, occurred, "at the height of [a] storm," Nature Herself raging against the injustice perpetrated upon humanity, presumably. Alas, this rather romantic statement is not factually supported by other primary-sourced, expert documentation. Online, historic Buffalo weather records are not yet fully available, but a search of extant physical resources reveal that original copies of daily weather data are maintained at the Buffalo Museum of Science. The entry for September 14, 1901, the day of McKinley's passing, reads in full:

> Partly cloudy day; slightly warmer; light to fresh variable winds. Early evening clear, followed by increasing cloudiness; rain began at 11.20 p.m. Comparative barometer readings taken to-day. A message was received from the Acting Chief of [the Buffalo Weather] Bureau at 2 p.m., directing all unnecessary work discontinue to-day and the day of the funeral, out of respect for the President, who died this morning.[4]

In any case, Mr. Penney maintained clippings until Czolgosz's trial, which was held on September 23 and 24, 1901, though the number of clippings begins to thin out on September 21, the last, most notable one detailing Czolgosz's execution on October 29. Admitting his guilt, Czolgosz was condemned to death after a one-hour deliberation, which focused mainly on his sanity. There are few additional articles after the trial itself, such as the Peter Thomas clipping, but their inclusion is often unclear. One described an astrologer who "predicted" McKinley's assassination, though its relevance, admittedly, escapes me. In short, though, why would prosecutor Penney record more on the topic if, indeed, these were his reference materials, preparatory for the trial that he was conducting?

As an archivist, I generally maintain the attitude that I can *provide* information but not necessarily *interpret* it for researchers, simply exhibiting as many primary sources, ancillary and supporting documents, and research avenues as I have available to students and other scholars. *But*, as an educator, it is my duty to sometimes guide researchers, underscoring discrepancies in reporting and asking them to step back and evaluate available reports based not only on their own knowledge but on the basis of context, social norms and expectations, and biases. As shown in above examples, "fake news," journalistic invention, and the desire to sell copy are lenses through which all data should be viewed.

World's fairs, dead presidents, or lawyers may not be of general interest to the public—but even in a source such as these scrapbooks, which are often explained as recording just those topics, there is a world of other data encoded inside them. These Thomas Penney Leon Czolgosz Trial Scrapbooks do not just capture the research material of a moment, but can open gateways into social mores, census and demographic material, population growth and urban studies, the treatment of marginalized populations, and meteorology, among other things. I have received excellent feedback using primary documents as a springboard to "unexpected" areas of study in this manner. There are surely many other subjects that can be opened even from this one resource, and any collection of this type will undoubtedly generate varied research avenues in a similar way.

## NOTES

1. Thomas Penney, "Leon Czolgosz Trial Scrapbooks," accessed May 1, 2019, https://www.worldcat.org/title/leon-czolgosz-trial-scrapbooks-1901-1911/oclc/775453194&referer=brief_results.

2. "McKinley Assassination Ink: A Documentary History of William McKinley's Assassination," (n.d.), accessed May 1, 2019, http://mckinleydeath.com/documents/govdocs/transcript.htm.

3. *Boston Daily Globe* Newspaper Archives (September 7, 1901), 4, accessed May 5, 2019, https://newspaperarchive.com/boston-daily-globe-sep-07-1901-p-4/.

4. Buffalo Weather Bureau [National Weather Service] Records, 1878–1948, Library, Buffalo Museum of Science.

# Chapter Three

# enLIGHTening the Past

## Corey Fabian-Barrett

In 2016, the Richardson Olmsted Campus was coming to the end of a long and challenging road. For the past decade, the abandoned National Historic Landmark had been studied by experts, stabilized by teams of engineers, and endlessly debated in community meetings, all with an eye toward finding new uses for the campus. And now, with the first redevelopment project coming to a close, it was finally time to celebrate. As one of the largest historic preservation projects in the nation, it was agreed that an equally massive event would be needed to thank the community for their support of the project over the past ten years.

Since the revitalization of the campus was truly a community-wide endeavor, the celebration was planned on the same scale. Drawing on what makes the campus unique, the event celebrated the site's transformation thus far, while providing new visitors with some historical context. How can free public events be leveraged to provide historical content? Is it possible to present history on such a large scale?

The event, called *enLIGHTen*, would eventually be held on the South Lawn of the Richardson Olmsted Campus on July 28, 2017. Featuring the Buffalo Philharmonic Orchestra playing in sync with original video art projected onto the Richardson Olmsted Campus's iconic Towers Building, *enLIGHTen* welcomed 15,000 people to the campus and explored the history behind the towers in a new way. The event melded together history, art, music, and architecture to create something exciting and engaging to celebrate the renaissance of the Richardson Olmsted Campus and of Buffalo itself.

From the start, *enLIGHTen* had two main goals: first and foremost, it was designed to be a community event that would welcome thousands to the revitalized campus, possibly for the first time ever. Second, given the opportunity to tell a story on such a large scale to so many new visitors, it was decided

Figure 3.1.  The original administration building of the Buffalo State Hospital, now home to the Richardson Olmsted Campus.
Image by Joe Cascio.

that the event would focus on the Richardson Olmsted Campus's often challenging history, a subject of fascination and misperception in the community.

Built starting in 1871 as the Buffalo State Asylum for the Insane, the buildings and grounds of the Richardson Olmsted Campus incorporated a system of enlightened treatment for people with mental illness developed by Dr. Thomas Story Kirkbride. The hospital was designed by the great American architect Henry Hobson Richardson with the famed landscape team of Frederick Law Olmsted and Calvert Vaux, creators of Central Park in New York City. The site was actively used as a state hospital until 1974, when the last patients moved into a more modern facility nearby. While the site was designated a National Historic Landmark in 1986, it remained largely abandoned and misunderstood for forty years.

During that time, the history of the Richardson Olmsted Campus became cloaked in mystery and rumor in the surrounding neighborhoods. Decades of overcrowding and then deinstitutionalization had preceded the hospital's closure in the 1970s. Thus, the living memory of the hospital amongst neighbors was extremely negative—no one remembered or knew about the hospital's earlier history as one of the most progressive asylums in the nation.

When the nonprofit Richardson Olmsted Campus was created in 2006, the organization was primarily charged with finding new uses for the abandoned hospital buildings and forty-two acres of grounds. But soon, the equally important role of history keeper and storyteller for the former asylum would emerge as a key part of the nonprofit's mission. As soon as was practical, the campus began offering historical tours.

By 2016, these standard tours had been going strong for three years, selling out every year and educating visitors about the long history of the site. But these tours were led by a small group of volunteers, which limited the number of tours offered and how many people could attend. With the first phase of redevelopment coming to a close, the organization saw an opportunity for a grand event that could shine a much brighter light on the site's history. While over ten thousand people had attended historical tours of the Richardson Olmsted Campus in the preceding years, this event would be a one-shot opportunity to reach that number—and, as it turned out, thousands more—in one night.

When it came time to choose what the event could be that would encompass all these lofty goals, it was clear that partnerships with other organizations would be critical. The Buffalo Philharmonic Orchestra, inspired by a recent video-mapped orchestra show in Cincinnati called "Lumenocity,"[1] approached the Richardson Olmsted Campus about doing something similar. It was perfect timing; the idea to use music and video-mapping together to tell the campus's story would push *enLIGHTen* into new, groundbreaking territory.

Video-mapping, a cutting-edge technology used at select sites around the world, charts the exterior of a building digitally to create a virtual, custom canvas for artists. Artists then work to design unique, moving images on the digital canvas. At the event, the digitally created art is projected onto the building, perfectly matching the outline and exterior of the structure, transforming the building itself. For *enLIGHTen*, the artists would have the additional challenge of syncing their video art to a live orchestra performance *and* projecting onto multiple facades of the building, as opposed to the more typical one-sided projection. To assist the artists, they were provided with a full musical program and recordings similar to how the orchestra intended to perform on the night of the show. Inspired equally by the Richardson Olmsted Campus history and by the musical recordings, the artistic team would build the visual parts of the show from the ground up.

To make this happen, the Richardson Olmsted Campus and the Buffalo Philharmonic Orchestra decided to work with an all-local team of artists and technicians. Buffalo-based artistic collective PROJEX agreed to create the video-mapped art that would illustrate the campus's history, and Buffalo Audio Visual was hired to provide the technology needed to project onto the massive buildings.

The name *enLIGHTen* was selected with a particular eye toward history. While in an obvious sense the event would be lighting up the Towers Building at the Richardson Olmsted Campus, the artistic story also aimed to enlighten visitors, encouraging them to think differently about the site's mental health care history. The original plan for the asylum—called "The Kirkbride Plan" after progressive physician Dr. Thomas Story Kirkbride—is widely considered one of the most enlightened therapeutic philosophies of the nineteenth century. The name *enLIGHTen* captured the spirit of the event *and* described the history of the place.

Once all partnerships were secured and a technical plan was in place, it was time to consider the creative aspects of the event. It was mutually agreed by all involved that creative decisions would be guided by the campus's history as the Buffalo State Asylum for the Insane. Accordingly, the classical program selected for the show featured only composers who lived with mental illness. The following nine movements were performed:

Movement #1—"A Royal Celebration"
Handel, Music for the Royal Fireworks Movement 1

Movement #2—"Beauty on the Inside"
Tchaikovsky, Waltz from *Swan Lake*

Movement #3—"Hundred Acres, featuring Charles Burchfield's work"
Satie, Gymnopedie #1

Movement #4—"40 Years Dormant"
Berlioz, Roman Carnival Overture

Movement #5—"Noodle in the Northern Lights Remixed"
Schumann, Symphony #2 First Movement

Movement #6—"A Beautiful Mind"
Rachmaninoff, "Vocalise"

Movement #7—"Radiant Beams"
Beethoven, Symphony #5 First Movement

Movement #8—"Symphony"
Mahler, Adagietto from Symphony #5

Movement #9—"Grande Finale"
Mussorgsky-Ravel, *Pictures at an Exhibition*, Hut on Fowl's Legs and Great
Gate

The video art created for *enLIGHTen* spoke more explicitly to the site's history, with each movement created by a different artist to tell one part of the campus's story. The first and last movements served as tributes to what the Richardson Olmsted Campus had become with celebratory visuals paired with majestic, triumphant music. The second movement focused on the design and architectural details found within the site, saluting the exceptional work of architect H. H. Richardson. The third movement used the art of Charles Burchfield, a prominent western New York artist whose work is currently housed in the Burchfield Penney Art Center directly adjacent to the campus, to highlight the working farmland originally part of the asylum grounds; working on the farm was an optional, but highly encouraged, form of treatment for patients of the asylum. The fourth movement explicitly illustrated the story of the campus's construction, use, and eventual decay, ending with the rebirth of the buildings. The remaining movements focused on mental health and illness, including artwork featuring a representation of neural pathways and two others focusing on the creativity often found in people living with mental illness.

In addition, certain historic guiding elements were selected to frame the overall story. These included the historic oak tree found on the South Lawn

**Figure 3.2.    The building's illumination captivates the crowd.**
Image by Joe Cascio.

of the campus and architectural details from inside the buildings, including the phoenix-like carving of a bird found on the grand staircase of the Towers Building. For the Richardson Olmsted Campus and the former state hospital, the bird symbolized rising from the ashes—for the buildings, it was a revitalization and rebirth as something new; for former patients, it was healing and a cure. The bird would serve as visual narrator throughout *enLIGHTen*, linking the movements and flying from piece to piece across the towers.

Richardson Olmsted Campus staff and volunteers worked for months with the artistic teams to make sure the history of the site was accurately represented in the final event's artwork. The artistic teams came on multiple tours of the site and spent time exploring historic photographs of the Buffalo State Asylum for the Insane in the campus's digital archive for inspiration. Staff provided tour scripts to the artistic teams and met with them on a weekly basis during the planning stages of the event to discuss each movement.

On the night of the event, however, all of the above detail was presented without a physical program or written context for the audience, a decision that would almost certainly change if the event happened again. Economic and environmental factors drove the decision to go without a printed physical program. A virtual program, including short essays about each movement and explanations of the program's connection to Richardson Olmsted Campus history, was made available online on a website dedicated to the event. However, no physical program or information was presented on the night of the event to attendees, leading most to assume that much of the artwork was merely pretty and not telling a specific story. This was a missed opportunity to underline the significance of the art created for the event and emphasize the importance of history.

Marketing and promotional efforts for the event took financial precedence over a printed program and the excellent opportunity to educate the public about the story behind the art. As mentioned above, there was an event website with extensive resources for those interested in learning more. Additionally, the Richardson Olmsted Campus, Buffalo Philharmonic Orchestra, and PROJEX all leveraged their social media in the weeks leading up to the event to promote and discuss the history behind the show. Media sponsorships from local newspapers, TV channels, and websites also helped with messaging.

Additionally, dozens of trained volunteer docents were on campus the night of the event to answer questions and engage with visitors about the history. These efforts experienced limited success; with many more people than anticipated attending the event, most volunteers ended up being crowd managers, not educators. For future versions of the event, it would be important to establish a pre-program history talk or provide dedicated tours for event attendees, rather than leave this vital interpretation up to chance amidst a crowd of thousands.

Ultimately, despite these challenges, *enLIGHTen* was a huge success for the organization. With just two opportunities to practice the whole show— once at an off-site rehearsal and once as a full dress rehearsal at the campus— the event went off beautifully. The hour-long program of art, music, and architecture ended up welcoming 15,000 people to the Richardson Olmsted Campus and symbolized a rebirth, not just for the formerly abandoned hospital, but for the city itself.[2]

Although the goal to tell the story of the Richardson Olmsted Campus through visual art may not have resonated with most attendees without supplemental information, the event itself ultimately helped the campus in much bigger ways in terms of name recognition and public profile. As a relatively new organization operating a very old historic site that had been known by many names throughout the years, the campus inherited a lot of name confusion. A big, splashy event like *enLIGHTen* did wonders to raise the profile of the Richardson Olmsted Campus in the community, directly leading to increased social media interaction and tags, positive feedback from visitors and neighbors, and widespread name recognition. No longer referred to as the "old psych center" or "state hospital"—now, everyone seemed to know the "Richardson Olmsted Campus."

Although *enLIGHTen* itself was a substantial production, this type of event is very scalable to the needs of any size institution thanks to the core idea that different kinds of art—music, visual art, and architecture—can come together to tell a bigger, historical story. This idea can be scaled down in any number of ways, including video-mapping that uses prerecorded music instead of a live orchestra, video-mapping one part of a building instead of multiple areas, or even simply projecting onto a wall or building instead of video-mapping it to create a precise video canvas.

The options abound, and adjusting the audience could also productively scale or change the event. *enLIGHTen* was an event for the general public

**Figure 3.3. *enLIGHTen.***
Image by Joe Cascio.

and celebration of meeting an operational milestone, so both the subject matter and the scale of the event were big and broad. By adjusting the topics or scale, the event can be made to suit much more specific groups. In particular, a smaller version of the event could be a fantastic student project, challenging high school or college-age students both intellectually and technologically.

With the increased attention generated by *enLIGHTen*, it has become easier to start conversations about the Richardson Olmsted Campus's history as the Buffalo State Asylum for the Insane and promote the various other history-based offerings at the campus. Based on frequent feedback from visitors demanding to know when *enLIGHTen* will be repeated, conversations have already begun to bring the event back to the campus in some capacity. Using the lessons learned from the first event, including the importance of providing a program and/or educational material about the event's content, a future version of *enLIGHTen* at the Richardson Olmsted Campus has the opportunity to be even better than the original.

## NOTES

1. "Lumenocity," Cincinnati USA Regional Tourism Network, accessed May 13, 2019, https://cincinnatiusa.com/events/lumenocity.

2. Select videos of the event are available in three episodes on YouTube: https://www.youtube.com/watch?v=rVESXkC2rJs&t.

# Chapter Four

# Art as History

## *Illustrating Your Community's Past*

### Michele Graves

Chartered in 2019, the Black Rock Historical Society (BRHS) serves four communities in the northwest section of the City of Buffalo, New York—Black Rock, Riverside, Grant-Amherst, and West Hertel. Physically located at 1902 Niagara Street in Buffalo, the BRHS is housed in a former storefront that was built circa 1890. The Niagara River and Erie Canal flow parallel and behind the historical society.

The Black Rock neighborhood got its name from a large outcropping of black limestone located in the Niagara River at a point where Massachusetts and Niagara Streets intersect. The rock ledge protruded 200 feet into the Niagara River, stood five feet above the waterline, and was about 200 feet long by 100 feet wide. It formed a natural eddy in the water, creating a small protected natural harbor downstream, serving to shelter small boats from river storms. It was blasted and pickaxed apart by Irish laborers in 1823 to make way for the construction of the Erie Canal that opened in 1825. Strata can still be seen today as you are driving north on the Interstate 190, after passing under the Peace Bridge and just past the Massachusetts Pumping Station.

As an institution focused on interpreting the past, situated in a thriving, diverse, and economically challenged neighborhood, the Black Rock Historical Society had to break out of the traditional norms of the historical society and static museum building. How could the BRHS engage its current constituents in caring about, and learning from, the rich history of this neighborhood and region as a whole? What methods could be employed to meet the community where they are? How could outreach opportunities be employed to share the mission of BRHS with those who may not be comfortable crossing the physical threshold of the historical society building? Using community engagement, BRHS set out to provide history where their constituents were not expecting it.

The *Art as History* project was born out of a firsthand experience by historian, artist, and Chair of the Black Rock Historical Society, Doreen DeBoth. While planning for the 200th anniversary of the War of 1812, DeBoth observed that while images were needed for promotional and educational materials, none existed of the Battle of Scajaquada Creek Bridge or the shipyard where Commodore Oliver Hazard Perry's five ships were outfitted. She researched both topics extensively by reading historical records and discussing these subjects with local historians. From her research, she began to sketch ideas of how these events may have appeared. This resulted in two, 2 × 4-foot paintings that were then used for posters, prints, museum exhibits, and publicity materials relating to the anniversary celebrations. Many historical events have no visual record. Prior to the nineteenth-century invention and widespread use of cameras and photographic equipment, historical events and places were depicted through the eyes of artists using paintings, drawings, lithographs, etchings, and sculpture to record history. DeBoth used both historical research and her artistic skills to create a visual representation of the past. She saw this process as an opportunity, an opening for students to learn history and be creative, resulting in the *Art as History* project. Art is a universal construct: it transcends language, cultural background, age, and ability. So much can be learned through the artistic process, including history. To be creative is to be human.

In order for the BRHS's idea to become a reality, partnerships were forged with other organizations in the city, specifically social service providers that were already committed to these targeted neighborhoods. The precursor to the *Art as History* project began in 2014 and was called *History in Your Neighborhood*. In collaboration with Buffalo schools and the West Side Youth Development Coalition (WSYDC), students were invited to participate in an essay competition. WSYDC is coordinated by the Institute of Community Health Promotions at the State University of New York Buffalo State College, and its mission is to improve the social, educational, health, family, economic, and community support for the pro-social development of youth. For the *History in Your Neighborhood* project, students were asked to research and write an essay about historical places and events in the Black Rock and Riverside neighborhoods; the winning essays were archived at the BRHS. The success of this project fueled the next stage of the program to go beyond the traditional narrative and encourage students to be creative in their depiction of history. The *Art as History* component was added in 2015.

Several goals were established for the *Art as History* project. As part of its mission, the Black Rock Historical Society is dedicated to preserving local history and educating the community. To align with this mission, *Art as History* utilizes an innovative method of teaching youth the link between local history, their community, and the visual arts. The goals for the student project include fostering a better understanding of neighborhood history, instilling pride in their community by learning how it has been shaped by the past, and feeling honored in having their work displayed publicly.

Annually at the start of the school year, BRHS staff and volunteers meet to determine the upcoming year's topic drawing from the historical society's collection and institution's mission. Past themes have included the following: Black Rock's History of Ships, Boats, and Planes; Envisioning the Scajaquada for a Better Future; Life on the Erie Canal; and Envisioning a Better Future—Neighborhood/Community. The project requires the commitment and support from the local school districts. Each September, principals of Buffalo's public, parochial, and private schools are sent letters describing the *Art as History* project and its guidelines. Students who participate must live in the targeted zip code areas of the west side of Buffalo. Not only does this support the mission of the BRHS, it is also a requirement of the funding support from WSYDC. In the letter, principals are asked to encourage their art and social studies teachers to participate in the *Art as History* initiative with their students.

Teachers who agree to participate have their students explore the annual theme in depth before transforming their historical understanding into a work of art. Students are provided with additional resources like the Black Rock Heritage Trail brochure and the Black Rock Historical Society newsletter, along with other relevant articles for reference. Teachers select the medium based on the topic, and financial support is provided for the purchase of appropriate and ample art supplies for entire classes to complete the project. Prizes are also purchased for the participating schools, which include art boxes containing drawing materials, sketch pads, canvases, brushes, pallets, and other art supplies. Each student who participates receives a certificate of community service. In order to raise the academic level of the project, local artists are enlisted to judge the works, such as Elizabeth Leader, environmental artist and children's book illustrator; Barbara Rowe, Professor of Fine Arts at Niagara Community College; and Doreen DeBoth, Chair of the Black Rock Historical Society.

For the majority of the student body in these community schools, with the exception of the building of the Erie Canal, much of Black Rock's history is not well known. Augmenting the curriculum with local history is one more way the BRHS forwards its mission with the younger generation. The Black Rock region has great diversity due to its growing immigrant population. It is generally a poor community with more than half the individuals living below the poverty level. It is composed of many different ethnic groups, and many of the student participants in the *Art as History* project are first generation or new arrivals to the United States and face language and cultural barriers. Many community members originate from the Congo, Sudan, Rwanda, Egypt, and other countries including China and Vietnam. Ethnic and racial groups include Hispanic/Latino, African American, Asian, Arabic, multiracial, Native American, and white. In addition to English and Spanish, other languages spoken include Karenni, Tigrinya, Arabic, French, Sudanese, Dinka, Madi, Mandarin, and Vietnamese.

For the *Art as History* project to be successful, it necessitated an understanding of the current composition of the Black Rock neighborhoods. English is not the first language of the majority of current residents in the area. Therefore, a special curriculum was developed by an English Language Learner (ELL) teacher in collaboration with an art teacher to help the students understand the project. To foster collaboration and participation, this newly developed curriculum is readily available and freely shared to all schools who participate in the program.

Through the *Art as History* project, students have shown through various mediums they can learn history without a command of the English language. By way of their art, they have expressed how to create and live in safe neighborhoods; envisioned an improved Scajaquada Creek; and depicted planes and boats from a bygone era. Their final projects show that creating art while learning about history can have a direct impact on their lives. Linking history with contemporary society resonates with students and stimulates their ideas by highlighting the importance of using the past to inform the future. The resulting artwork is a testament to the local schools' student involvement and commitment to the project. Their serious and enthusiastic approach was evident in how the students used color, line, and space to communicate their ideas.

For example, in the inaugural project that took place in 2015, the theme was Black Rock's History of Ships, Boats, and Planes. Students could choose to focus their work on the Black Rock Canal, the Black Rock Train Station, or the Curtiss Aeroplane Factory—all of which have a rich history and hold importance, not only in Buffalo, but for the entire country. An art teacher expressed his enthusiasm for the project:

> It has been my great pleasure to work with our sixth grade students and the Black Rock Historical Society, in collaborating to create art that is not only representative of our students' enormous artistic and creative potential, but that is also reflective of the historical significance of the Black Rock and Riverside communities. Our students did not disappoint.

The annual theme in 2016 asked students to take a closer look at Scajaquada Creek and Scajaquada Expressway. For this theme, one of the

Figure 4.1.   "Envisioning the Scajaquada," award-winning submission to the
*Art as History* program.
Courtesy of the Black Rock Historical Society.

school principals described her view about the *Art as History* project and its student impact:

> This project allowed our students to have a much better understanding of the Scajaquada Creek, what it was and what it could be in the future with the cleanup and plans for restoration. In order to build up the students' background knowledge, including that of the English Language Learners that never experienced art or ever painted before, [the teachers] incorporated elements of local art, public art, Greek Mythology. They even reached out to the Buffalo Niagara Waterkeepers for information about the kind of fish that will be reintroduced to the Scajaquada Creek after clean up. Projects like this really allow the students to gain a deeper understanding of the subject and a greater appreciation for their local community. Through this project we saw students who were reluctant to participate become confident and proud of their work and eager for more.

At the one local school, students in grades six through eight looked at both the Scajaquada Creek and the Scajaquada Expressway. They became further enamored with the topic and realized the close proximity to their school. Students utilized the available technology like iPads to improve their research skills and worked several weeks looking at the similarities and differences of the waterway and highway over time. The students were asked to illustrate and write a composition for what they envisioned for the creek or the expressway. According to judge Doreen DeBoth, "The explanations that accompanied the paintings showed that students had a genuine concern for the current condition of the creek and what could be done to improve air and water quality. Also, it was unanimous that community involvement was necessary to make it beautiful."

In 2017, the *Art as History* theme was Life on the Erie Canal to celebrate the 200th anniversary of the start of the canal's construction. The theme gave students an opportunity to explore the nearby canal history and to envision how it looked in the past. Students were provided with BRHS brochures and an Erie Canal coloring book. Three schools participated in this initiative, and for the first time fourth grade students were included as the Erie Canal is part of the state social studies curriculum. According to their teacher, "Students loved learning about the Erie Canal! The kids were very excited to do this project!"

The next year, the *Art as History* theme was Envisioning a Better Future—Neighborhood/Community and included the previous year's schools. Teachers were enthusiastic about participating again. One returning teacher added an essay element to the work of art in which her students researched and wrote about their local neighborhoods.

The success of the *Art as History* project is due in large part to the teachers who have embraced the concept. One teacher in recent years created an awards assembly for the contest winners and their families. The art was put on display, and photographs were taken of award winners and their families during the school-based ceremony. The awards assembly for the project has

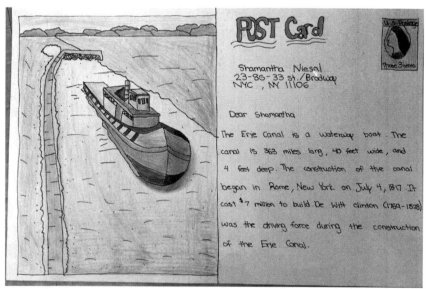

Figure 4.2. "Digging the Erie Canal," award-winning submission to the *Art as History* program.
Courtesy of the Black Rock Historical Society.

been important in providing positive peer involvement and for motivating students to become involved in their community in the future.

To date, more than a thousand students in grades four through twelve have participated in this initiative. Teachers have been instrumental in its success. They have embraced the program beyond the initial scope of the *Art as History* contest by developing a special ELL curriculum, taking field trips to study the subject matter, assigning essays to accompany the artwork, promoting the program to new schools, and planning award assemblies.

As we enter the planning stages for our sixth year, we continue to grow, evolve, and adapt the program. Building on the success of prior years, we continue to partner with WSYDC and others to underwrite the costs associated with a project of this magnitude. While it may be comforting for a small historical agency to stay within the walls of their building, it is through programs like *Art as History* that the next generation of neighborhood champions are born. It is our mission to share the rich history of Black Rock with a wide and diverse audience; after all, it is that diversity that built us in the first place.

## Chapter Five

# Vintage Game Nite @ the TR Site

## Lenora Henson

*Play should never be allowed to interfere with work; and a life devoted merely to play is, of all forms of existence, the most dismal. But the joy of life is a very good thing, and while work is the essential in it, play also has its place.*

—*Theodore Roosevelt[1]*

The Theodore Roosevelt Inaugural National Historic Site (TR Site) is a historic house museum that preserves the home of Ansley Wilcox, a Buffalo lawyer who hosted Roosevelt's 1901 inauguration following President William McKinley's assassination. Occurring in the aftermath of tragedy, Roosevelt's inauguration demonstrates the resilience of the American nation and its democracy. The simple ceremony reminded the country and the world that a peaceful transfer of power was possible, even after violence. Roosevelt went on to create what many have called the first modern presidency in US history.

For many years, the visitor experience at the TR Site was largely defined by guided tours, K–12 programming, or fundraising events (luncheons, fashion shows, etc.). In 2015, we launched a new public programming initiative. Among other things, it was our hope that this initiative would engage more diverse audiences and encourage repeat visitation. For the first time in our nearly fifty-year history, we introduced regular evening hours "Tuesday Nite @ the TR Site." Within that framework, our original programmatic offerings included *TRivia Nite* and *Speaker Nite*, both of which take place on a monthly basis from February to November. *Vintage Game Nite* was added to the mix approximately two years later and takes place four times a year.[2]

*Vintage Game Nite* offers a series of board, card, and parlor games from the turn of the twentieth century. Inspired in part by a similarly named program offered by the President Woodrow Wilson House (Washington, DC), the TR Site's *Vintage Game Nite* is designed to be an experiential learning opportunity that allows participants to better understand the changing values of the late nineteenth and early twentieth centuries, as reflected by the games themselves. It leveraged existing collections research as well as work that had been done when developing an exhibit centered around Roosevelt's 1913 autobiography. Further, it sought to capitalize on the successful balance between education and entertainment that had already been achieved with *TRivia Nite.*

Although it has been suggested that *Vintage Game Nite* could be modified for different audiences (e.g., families or teens), the program—as developed— is intended for adults. In particular, promotional efforts seek to target members of the Millennial generation (individuals born between 1981 and 1996) as well as Generation X (individuals born between 1965 and 1980).[3] Given the widespread appeal and relatively low stress involved in play, the appeal of *Vintage Game Nite* is reasoned to be broader than with the high(er) stakes and pressure of *TRivia Nite.*

On the "edutainment" spectrum, *Vintage Game Nite* falls much closer to the entertainment end of the scale. Since it also targets new audiences that may not have prior knowledge of the TR Site, our first learning goal is for participants to leave with a basic understanding of why Theodore Roosevelt is associated with this private-home-turned-museum. Beyond that, our goal is to encourage consideration of how various games reflect the concerns and values of the societies that develop, popularize, and play them. It is our hope that, after reflecting upon what the games offered at *Vintage Game Nite* tell us about society at the turn of the twentieth century, participants will also step back and think about what values are illuminated by today's popular games.

Many seemingly disparate elements came together to create *Vintage Game Nite @ the TR Site.* Long before the programming initiative began, Megan Hahin, former intern and current Executive Director of the Herschell Carrousel Factory Museum, digitized and catalogued a collection of Wilcox family letters and diaries; one of the themes that emerged from her work was the family's regular enjoyment of card and board games. For example, in one memorable letter, Ansley Wilcox gives his wife a lengthy list of tips and strategies for winning her next game of whist.[4] Family members are also known to have played Go Bang, checkers, backgammon, and Stops.

Although Theodore Roosevelt is generally associated with more strenuous pursuits, his autobiography and diaries reveal he enjoyed all manner of games as well. When recounting his first night in the Dakota Territory in 1883, for instance, Roosevelt describes playing "[O]ld [S]ledge round the table." On that particular occasion, his game was "interrupted by a frightful squawking which told us that a bobcat had made a raid on the chicken-house"—a scenario that *Vintage Game Nite* participants are hardly likely to face.[5] Other writings indicate the twenty-sixth president also enjoyed playing cribbage and backgammon.

When it came time to expand the "Tuesday Nite @ the TR Site" repertoire, this existing research, along with an awareness of the Woodrow Wilson House's Vintage Game Night, suggested exciting possibilities. One of our first steps was to reach out to the Wilson House, which led to a very gracious conversation with Sarah Andrews, Manager of Marketing and Special Events. She very helpfully shared not only some of their lessons learned, but also provided some sage advice on particularly engaging period games.

Developing a comprehensive program plan was our next major challenge. We were lucky to connect with an extraordinarily capable intern in the form of Christine Bacon, now Interim Director of Education at the Niagara Falls Underground Railroad Heritage Center (whose work is also featured in this volume). She began by researching and identifying games that could be included in the TR Site's version of *Vintage Game Nite*. We asked her to take a number of factors into consideration while developing her list. For example, we identified four broad categories of games that we wanted to focus on: (1) those played by Theodore Roosevelt, such as Old Sledge; (2) those played by the Wilcox family, such as whist; (3) those with subject matter relating to Theodore Roosevelt or his presidency, such as the 1899 board game Roosevelt at San Juan; and (4) those that, while having no direct connection to Roosevelt or the Wilcoxes, were clearly popular between 1901 and 1909, such as Pit.

Another consideration was the TR Site's ongoing effort to link its public programming to five issues that are introduced during our "standard" guided tour. Selected in part through a process of front-end audience evaluation, these issues (immigration and urban poverty; race and social equality; environmental conservation; big business and labor; as well as the US role in global affairs) are noteworthy in that Theodore Roosevelt faced them during his presidency, but they continue to be extremely relevant in today's world. Among the games that eventually came to be offered at *Vintage Game Nite*, the Big Stick Puzzle connects to Roosevelt's trust-busting efforts, while Jungles: The Great Hunting Game highlights Roosevelt's 1909 African safari and, by extension, raises questions about conservation practices.

Yet another consideration, brought to our attention by the folks at the Woodrow Wilson House, was how we expected *Vintage Game Nite* to unfold in terms of logistics and engagement. Because we wanted to encourage interaction among participants, we sought out games that could be played with multiple players and also varying numbers of players. Since we wanted participants to spend most of their time actually playing and also wanted them to have the opportunity to try more than one game, we looked for games that were relatively simple to learn and had a running time of forty-five minutes or less. As such, although both Roosevelt and the Wilcox family played chess, it did not make our short list of games. At the same time, we did bend these guidelines to include Bull Moose, a contemporary game based on the election of 1912. We're nothing if not flexible (sometimes).

At some point in the process, we also reached out to our colleagues at Sagamore Hill National Historic Site and Theodore Roosevelt Birthplace National Historic Site. Both suggested several games based on their collection holdings.

The resulting list was prioritized, and a record was created for each game. All entries include information about the game's genesis, its connection to Roosevelt or the Wilcoxes (if applicable), as well as a set of rules and related resources. When appropriate, ideas about how best to roll out a specific game in the context of *Vintage Game Nite* are also included. In some cases, the records also include images of the game. In all, approximately twenty-five games were identified as possibilities for inclusion.

The next challenge was acquiring games. Grants from M&T Bank as well as the New York State Council on the Arts provided funds that allowed us to develop our game collection. Some games—like Go Bang and Reversi—can be played using easily obtainable standard checkerboards. In several cases, we then created game pieces by spray-painting wooden discs (1-inch diameter) that can be found online or at a local craft store. For games like backgammon that have not changed in any significant way in the last century, we simply acquired a modern edition.

We found several complete early versions of Pit on eBay and Etsy. In other instances, we used the same websites to cobble together various elements of a single game. For example, we knew there was a circa 1912 edition of Parcheesi in Sagamore Hill's collection; we were able to buy the game board separately from the period-appropriate game tokens and dice.

When original games were unavailable or prohibitively expensive (we had a budget, but it had limits!), we searched for copies held in museum collections and worked with them to obtain high-resolution digital files; we then reproduced the games for use as part of *Vintage Game Nite*. This strategy enabled us to acquire or re-create, among others, The Game of Rough Riders (1890), The New Game of Hunting (1904), Jungles: The Great Hunting Game (1910?), and The Big Stick Puzzle (date unknown).

As the work of acquiring games was going on, we were also developing other important elements of the *Vintage Game Nite* program. A local craft brewery, Flying Bison Brewing Company, agreed to co-sponsor *Vintage Game Nite* and provide a selection of popular beers. At the suggestion of the Woodrow Wilson House, we also researched period-appropriate snack options to lend an added sense of authenticity to the evening. This also allows us to incorporate some interpretation at the snack table; participants will find, for example, a small sign explaining Theodore Roosevelt was president when Hershey's Chocolate Company introduced individually wrapped candies called Kisses in 1907[6] in front of a bowl of the chocolate treats. Ultimately, our food choices are practical on several levels: they need only minimal prep time, they are low grease (which helps to protect the games from greasy fingerprints), and they reinforce the low-key and casual atmosphere suggested by our tagline "Happy Hour Meets Vintage Gaming."

*Vintage Game Nite* participants choose games from an annotated "menu." For example, under the heading CARD GAMES, the listing for Jungles: The Great Hunting Game reads as follows: "Featuring animals, people & places from TR's post-presidency African safari. | 4, 6 or 8 players | 30–45 minutes." Likewise, under BOARD GAMES, the listing for backgammon reads: "In a diary entry from 1883, TR wrote, 'I can imagine nothing more happy in life than an evening spent in my cosy [*sic*] little sitting room, before a bright fire of soft coal, my books all around me, and playing backgammon with my own dainty mistress.' | 2 players | 30–60 minutes." Once participants choose a game to play, they are given a set of rules that have been transcribed by TR Site staff. Transcriptions were deemed necessary after finding that the printed rules that came with period games tended to be on the verge of falling apart. Retyping the rules ensured that they were readable and also enabled us to include additional historical context for each game. Meanwhile, table tents on each game table paint a broad story of an increasingly urban and industrial world during the late nineteenth and early twentieth centuries, a world where the center parlor table no longer needs to serve as the center of economic activity. Societal changes transform the parlor into a place for education, entertainment, and moral enlightenment—a perfect storm that allowed board games (which were touted as providing these benefits) to skyrocket in popularity.

In addition to the text-based interpretative elements, staff and volunteer facilitators create opportunities for participants to ask questions, make connections, and engage with the historical foundations of the games on an informal, as-needed basis. Our popular "Teaching Table"—where we focus on teaching one game per night—allows for these types of interactions in a more structured format. From our perspective, these conversations are also a chance to evaluate the individual games as well as the overall program on an informal basis. For instance, it was during one of these conversations that a participant

**Figure 5.1.   Selection of the games played during *Vintage Game Nite* @ the TR Site.**
Courtesy of the Theodore Roosevelt Inaugural Site Foundation.

memorably described the Game of Rough Riders as "just like Candy Land, but with a Bermuda Triangle–thing going on in the middle."

Before the TR Site officially debuted *Vintage Game Nite*, we held a free test run, with the understanding that participants would fill out an extended evaluation survey at the conclusion. This provided valuable insights and shaped our thinking on several elements of the program. For example, based on comments received, we sought out a more period-appropriate music playlist for the evening. We also took this feedback into account as we determined the pricing structure and added more games.

A shortened version of the original evaluation survey is available at every *Vintage Game Nite*. These surveys ask the following questions: (1) Is this your first time visiting the TR Site? (2) How did you hear about *Vintage Game Nite*? (3) How would you rate your overall experience this evening [Scale of 1 to 5; Poor to Excellent]? (4) How likely are you to return for another *Vintage Game Nite* [Scale of 1 to 5; Not at All Likely to Very Likely]? (5) How likely are you to recommend *Vintage Game Nite* to a friend [Scale of 1 to 5; Not at All Likely to Very Likely]? Participants also have the option to leave specific comments and/or suggestions.

Currently, *Vintage Game Nite* typically takes place on fifth Tuesdays at the Theodore Roosevelt Inaugural Site. The doors open at 5:30 p.m., and the event is open to adults age 21 and older. Admission is $10 per person or $5 for TR Site members and teetotalers. Admission includes one free drink, snacks, and a selection of all-you-can-play vintage games. Further information is available on the website at www.trsite.org.

With the current *Vintage Game Nite* structure as a model, we have considered a number of variations to appeal to different audiences. A *Vintage Game Nite* designed for families is an obvious opportunity. Participants have also suggested that homeschool groups might be an eager audience for this type of programming. Another option is to have themed nights, where a specific game is highlighted, and everyone learns that game. The possibilities are seemingly endless.

As of this writing (mid-2019), we have a bit more than a year of *Vintage Game Nite* under our proverbial belts. Attendance is trending upward slowly, and the feedback we are receiving is generally positive. For example, some participants have suggested that more facilitation is needed. But, when asked to describe *Vintage Game Nite* in three words or less, responses ranged from "Historically hysterical" and "Entertaining, laughs, learning" to "Nice night out" and "A good time." It is certainly a work in progress, but one that we feel is worthwhile given its ability to provide "a fascinating window on the values, beliefs, and aspirations of a nation undergoing tremendous change."[7]

## NOTES

1. Theodore Roosevelt, *Theodore Roosevelt: An Autobiography* (New York: Charles Scribner's Sons, 1923), 40.

2. "Tuesday Nite @ the TR Site" programming operates on a monthly cycle wherein *TRivia Nite* happens on the third Tuesday of most months; *Speaker Nite* takes place on the fourth Tuesday of most months; and *Vintage Game Nite* occurs when there is a month with a fifth Tuesday.

3. Michael Dimock, "Defining Generations: Where Millennials End and Generation Z Begins," Pew Research Center (January 17, 2019), accessed May 12, 2019, https://www.pewresearch.org/fact-tank/2019/01/17/where-millennials-end-and-gen eration-z-begins/.

4. Ansley Wilcox to Cornelia Coburn Rumsey Wilcox (September 5, 1879), in the collection of the Theodore Roosevelt Inaugural Site Foundation (Buffalo, NY).

5. Roosevelt, *Theodore Roosevelt: An Autobiography*, 95.

6. "Our Hershey's Happiness History | HERSHEY'S," accessed May 15, 2019, https://www.hersheys.com/en_us/our-story/our-history.html.

7. Margaret K. Hofer, *The Games We Played: The Golden Age of Board and Table Games* (New York: Princeton Architectural Press, 2003), 13.

## Chapter Six

# Learning History
# One Family at a Time

## Suzanne Jacobs

Is it possible to learn history by doing chores or playing games? Well, at the Hull Family Home & Farmstead, you can. At the yearly summer camp program, *History Camp for Kids,* children experience early 1800s life on the farm by doing pioneer chores like candle dipping, tin punching, weaving, and preparing a meal, as well as playing games like lacrosse. Following in the footsteps of generations before, participants use a combination of reenactments, site-based learning, and immersive experiences to learn about nineteenth-century life on the Niagara frontier.

The Hull Family Home & Farmstead was established more than two hundred years ago on property at what is now 5976 Genesee Street in Lancaster, New York. Warren Hull, a veteran of three enlistments in the American Revolution, had fought in New York State between 1779 and 1781. From a Connecticut family of farmers, he realized that land in this state was superior for agriculture. In 1804, he purchased an article, similar to a deed, for an acreage in the Town of Clarence from the Holland Land Company. Today this land resides within the contemporary boundaries of the Town of Lancaster, a suburb of Buffalo.

Warren Hull traveled to western New York from Connecticut with his wife, Polly, and their children. Along the way, they stopped in several counties in New York and worked at various farms, while their family grew to include ten children. After arriving in Clarence in Erie County and purchasing their own land, Warren and Polly probably constructed a log cabin on the property. Two more children were added to their family in 1805 and 1808. Over the next several years, the Hull family created what became a successful farm and orchard, specializing in crops of wheat, corn, and oats.

At the same time, circa 1810, Warren and Polly Hull constructed a large, Federal-style house in a very prominent location on the property. It faced the

**Figure 6.1.   Campers engage in period chores.**
Courtesy of the Hull Family Home & Farmstead.

Batavia Road (currently Genesee Street), a "thoroughfare" of close to fifty miles that travelers took between Buffalo and Batavia. One provision of the article they purchased was they had to open their home to travelers and provide a comfort station with food and rest for both people and horses.

The last Hull family members lived in the house until 1857. Subsequently, it was sold to and occupied by others. In 1991, however, the house was lost to its owner when he neglected to pay the required taxes. It was then purchased by a preservation group, the Landmark Society of Western New York, and a committee was formed to begin plans for its restoration.

In 1993, the Hull House was listed on the National Register of Historic Places, and it is also a New York State Historic Site. The restoration process began in early 2002, with structural stabilization, roof repair, and window replacement—all performed with the goal of maintaining authenticity in every aspect. After more than a dozen years, the exterior and interior restoration of the house is complete, as well as that of the family cemetery. The current focus is on the development and interpretation of the farmstead.

The mission of the Hull Family Home & Farmstead is to educate visitors about family and farm life on the western New York frontier in the early 1800s before construction and operation of the Erie Canal. The property is spacious, and most programs take place outdoors. A large double tent is erected for large group gatherings, lunches, and other activities. A kitchen garden has been constructed; further plans include the reestablishment of a small orchard and crops, outbuildings, and a threshing barn. Eventually, there will be a selection of the kind of animals the Hulls would have kept. More than $1.5 million in grants has been acquired to support the restoration of the Hull Family Home & Farmstead. Over the course of the last several years, the acreage has grown from one to twenty-eight. The adjoining Victorian house was purchased to support the many activities that benefit the foundation's mission. Parking areas and land for an eventual Education and Visitor Center are part of the farmstead.

The Hull Family Home & Farmstead operates under the auspices of the Hull House Foundation. The foundation was incorporated as a 501(c)(3) in 2006, and it was granted a charter from the Board of Regents of the New York State Department of Education in 2013. There is a ten-member board of directors that guides the work of the foundation. These individuals have skills in the fields of finance, education, law, and history. Theirs is primarily a fiduciary responsibility, searching for funding to continue growing the project and monitoring revenue and expenditures. There is no paid staff at the Hull Family Home & Farmstead; even the president and executive director of the foundation has never been paid. The staff of dedicated volunteers, however, did not wait for the completed restoration of the house to begin welcoming

Figure 6.2.    The Hull Family Home & Farmstead.

visitors to the site. Educational and public programs have been held on-site for several years, even as restoration work was still taking place. School field trips, open houses, and Revolutionary and Civil War reenactments and encampments have all been ongoing for ten years or more. One of these successful programs heading into its twelfth summer is *History Camp for Kids.*

In 2006, a group of Hull House volunteers visited similar historic homes in the region on a benchmarking trip. They were interested in studying the architecture, interpretive plans, and programming in homes contemporaneous with the Hull House. They were inspired when learning about a history camp sponsored by one of these homes and believed it would be an ideal project for the Hull Family Home & Farmstead. The education committee that had been established began planning, and the first history camp took place in 2008. *History Camp for Kids* operates for one week each summer, Monday through Friday from 9:00 a.m. to 4:00 p.m. daily.

It was determined this camp should be built around the Hull family stories and be an active, hands-on experience for campers. Using the Hull family to teach about the national narrative allows campers to experience history through the lens of a local family that they can relate to by living and working in their actual home. Brainstorming sessions took place; a list of ideas for presentations and activities was eventually culled down to what was achievable. Experts were approached to share their knowledge; Hull House volunteers found information that would help create meaningful activities in which campers could participate. Eventually a theme emerged for each day, and a schedule was created. Each year, the schedule may be tweaked, or a new or different presenter or activity added or substituted, but the original formula has worked very successfully.

As many of the presenters are teachers, they have expertise in setting goals, providing background knowledge, giving campers as much hands-on experience as possible, and assessing outcomes. This occurs with every activity, but it also occurs on a more global basis, as each day of camp begins with the Big Question for the day, an introduction to the day's theme, and the schedule of supporting activities.

The Big Question for the first day is, "Which is an easier life for a child, the life of a child in 1820 or the life of a child today?" Campers begin the week with an hour-long tour of the house, with presentations by first-person interpreters, volunteers adorned in period dress representing Hull family members. The Hull Family matriarch, Polly, guides them through the first floor of the house, explaining how she and Warren came to live there and how technologically advanced their house was, as evidenced by the Rumford fireplaces installed in each room and the up-to-date farm equipment used. Polly also talks about her family and their involvement in the War of 1812.

Rebecca, a Hull daughter, interprets the second floor. She invites children to lie on the beds with straw ticks, then passes raw wool, flax, soap, and other articles for them to touch and handle. Rebecca shows them an 1820 American flag and discusses the flag's design and the significance of having only fifteen stars and fifteen stripes. She tells them the story of the penning of the poem that became the "Star-Spangled Banner." It is not unusual to hear the campers sing the anthem, once they realize that the poem became a song—and one that they know. Miranda, another Hull daughter, leads the campers through the basement kitchen, which houses the original beehive oven. Miranda shows, explains, and passes around many kitchen items used for daily chores in the home: sugar cones, root vegetables, butter churn and paddles, irons, candle molds, and much more. After the tour, campers experience pioneer chores. They rotate through sweeping and emptying chamber pots; laundry and rug beating; fence building; carrying water and wood; and caring for animals. In the afternoon, they learn stenciling and tin punching, crafts used to decorate a house. The day concludes with a Revolutionary War reenactor, who discusses the causes of the war and the role of the patriot soldier.

The theme of the second day of camp is textiles, and the Big Question asks, "What are the differences between the fabrics of 1820 and today's fabrics?" Campers learn about natural fibers and compare them to modern synthetic fabrics. They have an opportunity to weave, sew a haversack, and make a lucet (a braided bracelet). A demonstration showing how the flax plant becomes linen is followed by campers practicing the process themselves. The final activity of the day is a stuffed mattress competition, whereby two teams race to empty a mattress, fill it with fresh straw, and sew the end, making sure there are no lumps!

Day three of camp features Native American culture, and the Big Question is, "What did the Haudenosaunee and other Native American nations contribute to white settlers?" Two residents of the Tuscarora Nation give a ninety-minute presentation, beginning with the Thanksgiving ceremony. They discuss traditions and beliefs and have many artifacts that campers examine and wear. Two Seneca Nation women teach campers how to make cornhusk dolls, and campers also have an opportunity to play lacrosse, a game inherited from Native Americans. Other activities on this day include a nature walk, emphasizing the plants that were used for medicinal purposes, and a presentation on corn and its multiple uses. The concluding presentation is about the War of 1812, with an emphasis on Native American involvement. Campers then experience a mock military drill.

Archaeology and trades are topics for the fourth day of camp, and campers are asked, "What do we learn from archaeology?" The State University of New York at Buffalo Department of Anthropology has been part of the site's restoration for many years. Their archaeologists conduct a dig on the premises in which campers participate. Campers learn how to excavate trenches, what each layer means, how to sift the soil, wash the finds, and catalog artifacts. They learn the significance of any artifacts found and what they tell us about the family and the time period under investigation. In a writing exercise at the end of the morning, camper teams are asked to create a story around a piece of china whose broken pieces they have re-assembled. In the afternoon, campers rotate through three stations: woodworking, tools, and the blacksmith. At the woodworking station, they fashion a hornbook, a tool used by school students in the nineteenth century. A hornbook is a wooden, paddle-like instrument on which students tack a piece of paper that contains a lesson they need to study or memorize. The paper is then covered with a thin, relatively transparent tissue made from a sheep's horn, hence the name. In the tool demonstration, a farmhand interpreter shows off his large collection of farm implements and construction tools of the time. He engages campers in corn grinding, carrying water in buckets on a yoke, sawing a log with a two-man saw, and many other hands-on experiences.

The theme for the final day of camp is about foodways, and campers are asked, "Is meal preparation easier today or in 1820, and why?" The primary activity of the morning, for which campers are dressed in period work shirts and aprons, is to prepare a meal in which everyone will share at lunchtime. They cut vegetables for stew, which is cooked over an open fire, and for veggie cakes. They cut up apples for applesauce, and they churn butter for the meal. Other activities include a fire-building demonstration and a seed quiz. The meal is preceded by a reading of etiquette rules from the time period. All campers participate in cleanup after the meal. Afternoon rotations include quill writing, completion of the hornbook, and a discussion about one-room schoolhouses. The final activity for camp is a presentation about the Erie Canal, which includes an outdoor reenactment of loading a canal boat and the singing of canal songs like the 1905 "Low Bridge, Everybody Down." The presenters are a middle school social studies teacher and a music teacher, who lead the campers in songs and accompany the singing on guitar.

The camp's success is a result of the many partners that are brought in to offer content expertise, as well as a diversity of presenters. Volunteer docents and camp organizers have researched and perfected their presentations and demonstrations, whether it be about textiles, stenciling, flax-to-linen process, quill writing, weaving, tin punching, lucet making, or a nature walk to learn about native plants.

It is also worth noting that campers are provided two daily snacks that would have been appropriate at the time: apples, carrots, cheese, beef jerky, three-sisters soup, corn bread, hardtack, or popcorn. On archaeology day, the snack is "dirt," in other words chocolate cookie crumbs. They are also given time to learn and play period games, both indoor and outdoor.

Throughout each day, campers are encouraged to be thinking about the Big Question. At the end of the day, they write their responses in their Reflection Journals. The Reflection Journal and the Big Question give campers time to think about the day's activities; provide them with an opportunity to compose ideas and write their own narrative; reinforce camp learning objectives; and, because they know they might have to read their responses aloud, encourage them to take the journal writing seriously and be thoughtful in their writing. To encourage critical thinking, it is important to have the campers comparing or contrasting and exploring cause-effect relationships. They are asked to support their opinions with facts. Each evening, a Hull House volunteer reads the campers' reflections and chooses several examples to be read aloud the next morning. Reviewing the responses allows the volunteer staff to be sure the campers are comprehending the themes and provides an opportunity to clarify or include additional information the following day.

Campers invited to attend *History Camp for Kids* are entering grades five through eight. It is preferred that they have studied local and New York State history in school, as outlined in the fourth grade social studies curriculum. Notifications about history camp are sent to local newspapers, posted in local libraries, and put in schools' electronic newsletters. Twenty campers is the target number, although more have been accepted. Most of the campers come from Lancaster and neighboring towns. They and their parents are aware that this site is a local attraction. Even if the campers are not from Lancaster, the point is made that this is a regional asset, and there is no place like it in western New York. Through the years, Lancaster High School students have volunteered to help on workdays; they acknowledge the site's importance to the town and region.

There are several ways we have assessed the effectiveness of the camp. At the end of the week, campers are asked to evaluate their overall experience. Their responses are always extremely positive. They are asked to tell what their favorite day was (most choose all), what activity they liked least, whether they would recommend the camp to friends, and any other comments. This last section of the evaluation is always positive, with many campers claiming they want to return. We have had several campers who have returned for a second, or even a third year. In addition, there is always a growing list of former campers who want to return as teen volunteers.

Parent feedback is also very positive. Each evening, parents are emailed photos of their children engaging in camp activities. This is an opportunity for them to discuss camp with their children and to react, either by email or during drop-off the next day. They are delighted to be included in this way, as evidenced by their comments when they drop their children off the next morning. Many would like a *History Camp for Adults* so they can have a similar experience! The possibilities for scaling are limitless.

Another means of assessing the effectiveness of camp is a debriefing session the education committee holds when camp is finished. In addition to reading the camper evaluations, a critical eye is focused on each day's schedule and activity. Committee members look for ways to improve the content of the activities, the timing and scheduling, and the outcomes. For example, the committee is always conscious of the length of presentations; it is important that most of the day be composed of interactive experiences. The comfort of campers has led us to change venues on the property, and we have learned that it is always necessary to have a contingency plan in case of rain.

The educational mission of the Hull Family Home & Farmstead centers on the stories that can be told through the Hull family. Their lives intersect with several significant eras in American history, such as the Revolutionary War, the War of 1812, the American Civil War, the building and opening of the Erie Canal, and westward expansion. The learning objectives for *History Camp for Kids* mirror the larger institution's goals and strive for campers to understand these local stories and how they relate to the bigger historical narrative. As campers weave their way through the Hull family tree, they learn that family members from each generation fought in a war, that the homeschooling of the twelve children by their mother led them to well-respected professions, and that many of Warren and Polly's twelve children and grandchildren moved west, making them part of the country's westward expansion and migration. *History Camp for Kids* utilizes the Hull family, their home, their community, and what their life would have been like to engage campers in history in a way they least expect.

*Chapter Seven*

# The Extinct Birds Project

## Jane Johnson, Twan Leenders, and Alberto Rey

*The truth of the matter is, the birds could very well live without us, but many—perhaps all—of us would find life incomplete, indeed almost intolerable without the birds.*

—Roger Tory Peterson (1908–1996)

The Roger Tory Peterson Institute of Natural History (RTPI) is located in Jamestown, New York, where famed naturalist, educator, and nature artist Roger Tory Peterson was born and inspired. RTPI, as an educational institution, is charged with preserving Peterson's lifetime body of ornithological-related work and making it available to the world for educational purposes. Included in the institute's archives is a collection of preserved bird specimens (museum study skins), which were acquired by Peterson to be models and reference material for his field guide art. Peterson considered himself to be, first and foremost, an artist. To achieve a more realistic interpretation of a species, he used these specimens as an artist's model. Although he was an authority on the specific bird species, he needed to study physical specimens to ensure scientific accuracy. This collection formed the inspiration for the *Extinct Birds Project,* where these seemingly lifeless specimens opened a dialogue between contemporary art, research, conservation, and education almost a century after their original use. Peterson saw one purpose for their collection; artist Alberto Rey saw inspiration for an exploration into their stories and the historical narrative that led them to the archival rooms of the RTPI.

While the staff and supporters of smaller regional museums or specialized research institutes are well versed in an organization's importance and role in society, smaller institutions have a harder time appealing to a wide, broad audience. Audience development and diversification is oftentimes a strategic goal of an organization. With limited resources, this lofty goal may seem un-obtainable. How, then, can smaller organizations utilize external partners to develop projects that increase the scale, reach, audience, and interest of their traditional visitor base? The *Extinct Birds Project* was an ambitious undertaking that resulted in multiple products that expanded the reach of RTPI and introduced new audiences to the collection, Peterson, and the work of Alberto Rey. Anyone who has interacted with the *Extinct Birds Project* in any of its forms—exhibition, publication, presentation, workshop, or online presence—may not have realized that they were also experiencing a history lesson. Artwork, study skins, and skillful narrative were woven together to present a seamless product that presented history where visitors were not expecting it.

Along with preserving Roger Tory Peterson's life's work, RTPI is also committed to continuing Peterson's legacy by providing programming that shares his commitment to education and conservation. Valuable biological data is continuously derived from historic museum specimens, and, in the case of Peterson's bird skin collection, the field guide plates created from these specimens have educated and inspired tens of millions of bird watchers and nature enthusiasts the planet over. The paradox of collecting wild birds to benefit conservation and education is powerful—particularly in the case of bird species that are now extinct. Should we collect biological specimens for natural history museums? How has this situation changed from times of natural abundance without legal protection for wildlife to our modern days of ongoing extinctions in spite of strict laws governing the collection of wild animals? The *Extinct Birds Project* provides a historical perspective on what happened to each of the extinct bird species featured, a biographical survey of each collector, and the role of politics in conservation practice over the last two centuries. Since the *Extinct Birds Project* started with a visit by Alberto Rey to the institute's special collections, it was the perfect venue at which to premiere this traveling exhibition.

Artist Alberto Rey took a behind-the-scenes tour of the Roger Tory Peterson Institute of Natural History's archives; the moment he laid eyes on the first extinct bird species, its cotton-filled skin made a lasting impression. Flooded with emotion, he was filled with questions: How did these skins get to this particular museum? How did the museum acquire the birds? Should the birds have been collected if the species was already exceedingly rare, to the point that it eventually became extinct? Where was each bird collected? What was its life like? Who collected the birds and how? What were the collectors thinking as they acquired the birds? What were the collectors' lives like? What was the process of preparing these museum skins to allow them to be preserved for more than a century in some cases? And why was he not as moved by the other birds in the collections he visited—those that are currently not extinct? From this visit, Rey wondered how he might create a body of work that would convey the emotions he felt and the questions he had when he first observed the extinct bird skins in the collection storage room. To increase the breadth of work, he also included some of the extinct bird collection from the Museum of Comparative Zoology at Harvard University for the project.

The *Extinct Birds Project* took approximately three years to complete. The project included two years of research and one year to produce the artwork; write, illustrate, and publish the book; and develop the website. For the first stage of the project, utilizing the collections at RTPI and Harvard University, seventeen extinct bird species were selected that represented various regions from around the world and had the appropriate associated data necessary for such an in-depth and multifaceted analysis. Rey was committed to creating a project that captured the emotions he felt when he saw his first extinct bird specimen. He carefully thought through the entire process and how each painting would be installed in an exhibition, long before he even picked up a brush. It was important to Rey to create paintings that inspired thoughtful interaction between the viewer and the finished works. He wanted the audience to, at first, be drawn to the aesthetic qualities of the extinct bird paintings and, then, to feel the tremendous sense of sadness and finality that he first experienced when he saw the bird skin. He believed the emotional connection between the audience and the extinct birds was critical to creating long-term sensitivity to environmental issues that had plagued these specific species and many others that are endangered or threatened. Eighteen paintings were created, one for each species with the exception of one that was represented by two paintings.

Rey realized the paintings alone could not tell the entire story, so he researched, wrote, and published a book that answered many of the questions he had when he first encountered the extinct bird skins. As with any research project, the questions Rey initially wanted to answer led him to other questions that were just as insightful as the initial pathway. And because the questions related to the environment and society, there were never any simple answers. To seek out these answers, Rey relied on various government agencies' reports, hard-copy publications, out-of-print scanned publications, and countless articles on related subject matter that brought different insights about the issues covered in the project. For an overview, he researched how birds were collected over the centuries and the politics in classifying birds as "extinct." Rey thought it was important to personalize each specimen he painted. Therefore, a great deal of research was undertaken about how and when the collector acquired the specimen, as well as biographical information about each collector, especially when the information was not widely known prior to this study.

Once the research was complete, the book was written in an accessible manner so that it would be available to a wide audience. After deciding on a publisher, a draft of the book was sent to Dr. Twan Leenders, Conservation Biologist and President of RTPI, to write the foreword, and to Dr. Stephanie Lewthwaite, Department of American and Canadian Studies at the University of Nottingham, United Kingdom, to write the conclusion. During this time, Rey made a list of illustrations needed for each chapter, and he began creating each one, using watercolor as the main medium. When everything for the book was ready, it was handed over to Jason Dilworth, a colleague of Rey's at the State University of New York at Fredonia. Dilworth designed the final publication, exhibit labels, and marketing items for the exhibition. RTPI contributed to the publication of the project's book. Additional funding for the publication and project was secured through the sale of some of the featured paintings before the book was published.

Another component of the *Extinct Birds Project* was a website to help promote the project, upcoming exhibitions, programming, and the publication. Since RTPI was where the inspiration and work for the project began, institute staff and Rey thought the exhibition should premiere there. Alberto Rey and Jane Johnson, Director of Exhibitions and Marketing, discussed the best ways to incorporate the RTPI collection into the exhibition and curated the exhibition together. The details about the preparation and analysis of the project are outlined further on the website.[1]

The *Extinct Birds Project* exhibition opened to the public on August 17, 2018, and remained on view at RTPI through January 20, 2019. The final exhibition included eighteen paintings, the extinct bird study skins from RTPI's collection, and audio recordings of extinct birds used as ambient sound in the galleries. Docent tours of the exhibit were offered for the community, environmental groups, and schools. Aside from the physical exhibition, the institute sponsored an artist's reception and provided journal drawing workshops, gallery talks, and book signings with Rey. Dilworth also gave a lecture and led a graphic design workshop. These types of programs allowed artists and designers to engage with the audience in ways that can only happen in person. For example, it provided the artist and designer an opportunity to answer questions about elements of the project they might not have been able to fully address through the static avenues of the exhibition, book, and website. It also allowed the viewer to learn more about the personal connection the artist and designer had with the content explored in the project.

The increasingly relevant topics of conservation and extinction within the *Extinct Birds Project* drew interest from a diverse audience. The exhibition itself, along with its programming, attracted ages ranging from elementary school students to older adults. Nature lovers, art enthusiasts, college students,

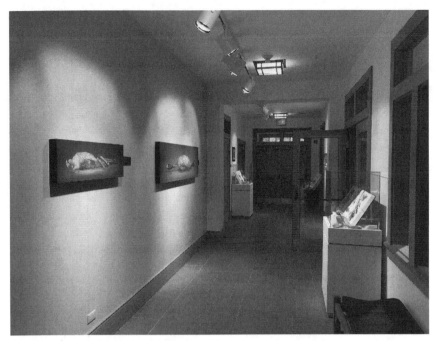

**Figure 7.1.** The exhibition installed at the Roger Tory Peterson Institute of Natural History, Jamestown, New York.
Image by Jane Johnson.

scientists, researchers, and others came to the institute to view the exhibit and experience both the sadness and beauty of this project. Rey's connection to his work for the project created enthusiasm and interest across all demographics, and his presence at RTPI programming throughout the exhibition was a bridge for visitors between the paintings themselves and the true meaning behind them. Significant impact was evident when, for example, art students from Jamestown Community College toured the exhibition with Rey, thus experiencing it through the artist's eyes. Reaching this demographic through this project was essential, and the hope is that this project was a gateway and the partnership will continue even though the exhibition has closed.

Regular social media updates (Instagram and Facebook) about the project were instrumental in securing new audiences and keeping the public informed and engaged throughout all its phases. Members of the public who normally do not attend museums or art galleries who came into contact with Rey during the project commented how much they appreciated the updates on social media. They felt it provided them insight into the process of creating the project and updates about the progress of the completed paintings. Using social media has proven to be an inexpensive but effective way of reaching a new audience because posts were made regularly and included a more personal perspective of the project.

Hosting projects at RTPI such as Rey's is an example of how far-reaching the interests and talents of a particular artist can be in relation to bringing current environmental and natural history issues to the forefront. Rey's project has given RTPI staff a chance to ponder what could be done differently in future collaborations with artists, as well as with Roger Tory Peterson's artwork itself. For example, more public programming and workshop offerings can be planned throughout an exhibition period to reach a larger number of visitors. Artwork featured in RTPI's galleries is intended to be used as beautiful public displays, but also as educational tools to bring awareness to specific environmental topics, and much more. When hosting a unique project such as Rey's or others, targeting a greater number of art, history, and science departments in local and regional high schools and colleges is essential. Marketing the particular project can and should begin in a timely fashion to allow educational institutions ample time to prepare for prospective field trips, lectures, workshops, discussions, and tours with the artist at RTPI.

Public reaction to the *Extinct Birds Project* demonstrated that Rey was able to convey current, historical, and scientific significance through his paintings and the accompanying publication. Visitors to RTPI's galleries recorded an array of thoughts in the visitor log. One visitor from Concord, Massachusetts, wrote: "The paintings are lovely—evocative—sad. Thank you for bringing back—in a different way—the beauty of these birds." A local resident recorded: "Exquisite and somber exhibit—Alberto is an incredible artist and his work and that of Roger Tory Peterson help us remember what has been lost and to hopefully better care for what remains." Another local visitor wrote: "Alberto Rey—a 'naturalist' painter of quality reminding us of natural beauty and wonder lost."

The *Extinct Birds Project* and RTPI received significant and positive press coverage in the western New York region. Media releases sent to regional newspapers throughout the exhibition period helped to give the project increased exposure. In addition, beautifully designed advertisements in publications such as the Cornell Lab of Ornithology's *Living Bird* magazine promoted the project to audiences interested in ornithological study. One example of positive media coverage included comments by Jennifer Ackerman, author of *The New York Times* best seller *The Genius of Birds*:

What a poignant and beautiful book. Alberto Rey catalogues seventeen birds that have vanished from the face of the earth—the Black Mamo and the Laughing Owl, the Pink-headed Duck, the Imperial Woodpecker, and the Paradise Parrot. In moving prose, he tells the stories of their lives and their demise, who

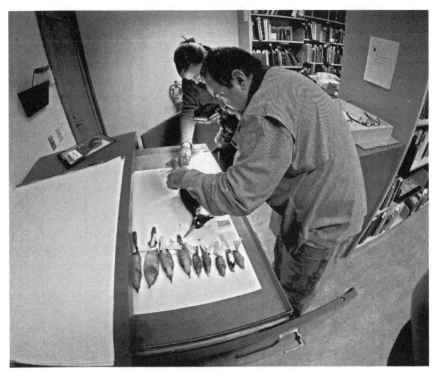

**Figure 7.2.    Alberto Rey and Jane Johnson work with the specimens at the Roger Tory Peterson Institute of Natural History.**
Image by Diego Rey.

collected the last remaining birds of their kind and why. And he memorializes their "small, lifeless, feathered bodies" in photographs and paintings so full of feeling they take your breath away. This is a book to keep around and to give to others, to remind us all of the disappearance of beloved bird species occurring all around us.[2]

Featuring the *Extinct Birds Project* at RTPI was just the beginning of a powerful initiative by Rey and others to share the sad and poignant subject of extinction. In continuing this initiative, Rey has recently collaborated with the State University of New York at Buffalo (UB) Art Galleries and the Buffalo Museum of Science to present two new exhibitions, *Alberto Rey: Lost Beauty I and II*, a two-part project featuring new work by the artist. *Alberto Rey: Lost Beauty I* was on view from June 8 to August 18, 2019, at UB Anderson Gallery. This exhibition showcased the *Extinct Birds Project*, including paintings and ceramics by Alberto Rey as well as extinct bird specimens, videos, and audio recordings from the Roger Tory Peterson Institute of Natural History;

Macaulay Library of the Cornell Lab of Ornithology, Cornell University, Ithaca, New York; and the Buffalo Museum of Science. The Buffalo Museum of Science will present the second part of this collaboration in summer 2020. *Alberto Rey: Lost Beauty II* will include a new body of site-specific work based on environmental issues and the museum's vast collection of artifacts and specimens collected since the early 1800s.

The *Extinct Birds Project* made complicated environmental and social issues accessible by combining Alberto Rey's artwork, publication, and website with RTPI's important mission and venue. The project provides the viewer with an emotional connection to issues of environmental change, extinction, mankind's role as stewards of nature, and the complexities of nature study. The historical perspective provides a background for understanding the factors that are still affecting many species across the globe and in local communities. Rey and RTPI believed that using artwork, a website, a print publication, and on-site programming provides diverse opportunities for an eclectic audience to engage with the work and participate in what could provide long-term educational benefits.

While it is true that not all small cultural organizations have such a rich collection to pull from or build upon like the scholarship of an environmental powerhouse like Roger Tory Peterson, this project is presented here as an example of the possibilities of partnership. Oftentimes it takes a new visitor, scholar, or artist to bring a fresh perspective to that which museum staff may have become complacent with. What we see daily sparks wonder in those who choose to explore. Be open to far-reaching and ambitious possibilities, as you never know where the idea for the next major initiative might begin.

As the late Roger Tory Peterson's 1934 *A Field Guide to the Birds* made nature accessible to a vast audience—from the nature novice to the experienced birders and naturalists—Rey's *Extinct Birds Project* made specific environmental issues accessible. Peterson was instrumental in driving the modern environmental movement; Rey's *Extinct Birds Project* carries on this mission.

*The philosophy that I have worked under most of my life is that the serious study of natural history is an activity which has far-reaching effects in every aspect of a person's life. It ultimately makes people protective of the environment in a very committed way. It is my opinion that the study of natural history should be the primary avenue for creating environmentalists.*

*—Roger Tory Peterson (1908–1996)*

# NOTES

1. Alberto Rey, *Extinct Birds Project*, www.extinctbirdsproject.com.
2. Jennifer Ackerman, Review of Alberto Rey's *Extinct Birds Project*, http://www.extinctbirdsproject.com/book.html.

*Chapter Eight*

# History in a Science Museum?

## Kathryn H. Leacock

History in a science museum? Certainly! Don't let the name of an organization or institution develop into a barrier for exploration. Many "science museums" house historic collections and archives that can be accessed to cover a wide range of subjects beyond those of the physical sciences. The Buffalo Museum of Science (BMS) is one such institution.

While the name Buffalo Museum of Science and many of its exhibits conjure mental images of Van de Graaff generators and hands-on interactive exhibits, a little digging into the museum's past reveals a wealth of topics available for historical inquiry. Conversely, not all activities conducted in a science museum need to be hands-on and interactive. Developing programming grounded in a historical narrative can provide mission-rich content to lifelong learners. At the Buffalo Museum of Science, previously ad hoc behind-the-scenes tours were framed into a suite of programs aimed at an adult audience. Replacing the sage on the stage presentations in the four-hundred-seat auditorium, these intimate tours provide historical narrative, behind-the-scenes collections access, program revenue, and conversations about current topics while exploring the past.

The Buffalo Museum of Science is operated by the Buffalo Society of Natural Sciences. In 1861, as collections and interest in the natural sciences grew, interested citizens decided to organize a Natural History Society. A paper was circulated throughout the City of Buffalo, New York, to see who might be interested in pursuing this venture. The signatures included that of former US President Millard Fillmore. The first president of the society was the Honorable George W. Clinton, son of four-term Governor of New York DeWitt Clinton, elected at the first meeting in 1861. While the museum building opened its doors on Humboldt Parkway in Buffalo, New York, in 1929, the society had already been in existence for sixty-eight years before curious visitors wandered the museum's halls.

Since its humble beginning, the museum has amassed a sizeable collection of more than 700,000 artifacts and specimens. As with most museums, only a small portion of this material is on view to the public at any one time. More specifically, the BMS's anthropology collection houses approximately 120,000 artifacts from across the globe and throughout time. With limited exhibition space, how can this rich resource be shared with the community? After all, these collections are stored in trust for the public; these are not private storehouses for the elite. As the BMS embarked on a new strategic planning process in 2017, constituents and community members were asked to weigh in on the museum's place in contemporary society. Increasing access to the collection was a reoccurring theme in the various focus groups that convened as part of the planning process. How can a museum increase access to their collection with limited public exhibition space? This led to a discussion about behind-the-scenes access. While tours of the "storerooms" have occurred for decades, these were limited to donor prospects, friends and family, and visiting researchers. How can these ad hoc tours be developed into a meaningful program that supports the mission and bottom line of the organization? The fear was that after a visitor came for a behind-the-scenes tour, what would motivate repeat visitation? How would we avoid the "been there, done that" mentality? We decided the tours had to be based on a specific theme and not just opening all the doors for a look-see. Themes provided the context, marketability, and desire to attend all the tours. It also allowed the content to remain fresh and permitted the marketing team to have new angles to entice visitors into the museum's dark hallways.

Our inaugural anthropology-based tours took a diversion from the scientific content of the permanent exhibits and explored the collection from a historical perspective. This first tour was entitled *The Pan-American Exposition—The Buffalo Museum of Science's Story*, fondly referred to as the *Exposition Tour*.

At the turn of the twentieth century, the United States reveled in a time of prosperity and growth. This innovation, invention, and national pride was shared with the wider audience through world's fairs and expositions. Although there were some fairs in Europe dating back to the eighteenth century, in the United States, the trend began with the Exhibition of All Nations in New York City in 1853. Since then, world's fairs and expositions have been held worldwide. These fairs were community events on a national scale.

In 1901, the Pan-American Exposition welcomed eight million visitors to the City of Buffalo in just seven short months (May 1 through November 2). This temporary "City of Light" came at a cost of $7 million ($216 million in 2019 dollars). At a time when a loaf of bread was five cents and a gallon of milk twenty-eight cents, visitors spent an average of twenty-five cents for general admission to the fairgrounds. Contrary to the belief of many Buffalonians, the Pan-American Exposition was not an isolated event, nor was it the first or last of its kind. The lasting effect of the Pan-American Exposition resides in Buffalo's cultural institutions. While many turn to the Buffalo History Museum or the Theodore Roosevelt Inaugural National Historic Site to learn all about this event, there are other institutions that can offer alternate points of view of this historic affair.

The Buffalo Society of Natural Sciences was approached by the Pan-American Exposition Company to be involved in presenting natural sciences at the fair. Not only did the society display its growing collections, including their collection of ethnographic pottery displayed in the Ethnology Building, they partnered with fair officials to bring the "African Village" to Buffalo. Controversial by twenty-first-century sensibilities, the African Village was an ethnographic village housed on the exposition's midway. The village was populated by a group of individuals from primarily West Africa, who were brought to Buffalo to inform visitors about life on the African continent. The participants in the African Village lived on the fairgrounds in structures they erected upon arriving in Buffalo. In addition to the people, their material culture was also exhibited in a small "museum" in the village area. As per the agreement with the Buffalo Society of Natural Sciences, at the close of the fair, the material culture was donated to the society and remains a major component of the museum's anthropology collection.

The goal of the African Village was consistent with the society's mission to educate. According to the promotional brochure produced for the exposition, people from eleven different tribes lived in this village, under the guidance of two African men—John Tevi and Ogolaurie—who served as its chiefs. Several different religions were practiced in the village, including Dahomeyan Vodun, animism, and Islam. Some of the villagers were accompanied by their families, including infants and children. Kinship ties appear to have linked some other members of the community. Photographs suggest that strong friendships developed within the village, but other sources record periods of tension.

While the fair opened to the public on May 1, 1901, the "Africans" didn't arrive until June. Images show them entering the exposition's midway on June 10 to the site of the African Village. They then had to construct their homes; the goal was to have "native huts built by natives of native materials."[1] Estimates have varied from early statements that 150 people would live in the village to as few as sixty people, identifiable in photographs from the time. Archival discoveries have allowed us to combine names from the passenger lists of ships that brought the villagers to America with oral histories. We can now identify eighty-six members of the village by name, place of last residence, and gender. We also have information on the roles, ages, and literacy of some of the village's members. They included musicians, dancers, weavers, jewelers, priests, chiefs, servants, and one man called a "rover."[2] There were men, women, and children. The youngest member of the village was just one year old; the oldest member was fifty-eight. At least thirty-six of the eighty-five village members could read. This compares well with the literacy rate in Buffalo around 1901.

Documentary evidence indicates that the African people came to the Pan-American knowing generally what to expect. They were paid to live and perform there. Several members of the group had appeared previously in world's fairs at Chicago (1893) and San Francisco (1894). One of these men, John Tevi, recruited the Dahomeyan performers and was one of two African "chiefs" in charge of the village. His story suggests that the Africans joined the troupe to see the world, make money, have an adventure, gain experience, and improve their lives.[3]

When the Pan-American Exposition closed in November 1901, the Buffalo Society of Natural Sciences acquired all the material from the African Village. More than 1,200 artifacts came to the museum, of which 527 still exist. This is the largest collection remaining from any of the African Villages that appeared in American or European world's fairs during the late nineteenth and early twentieth centuries. That said, the Pan-American story is not interpreted in the current public exhibition space at the museum. While it is of local significance, its historical narrative does not align with the museum's current interpretive plan. Rather, the museum's current anthropology offering deals with looking at cultures across time and place, highlighting the similarities between peoples. The anthropology collection is showcased in the exhibit *Artifacts*, which is more akin to an Anthropology 100 course. While some African Village materials are displayed as illustrations of the artistic traditions of turn-of-the-century West Africa, the lens is the object, not how it arrived in Buffalo.

Providing visitors with behind-the-scenes access to the Pan-American collection as a whole allows the facilitator to provide historical content in an intimate setting, giving access to this otherwise hidden narrative. While the tour is grounded in viewing the artifacts and ephemera from the African Village, the informal setting allows for conversations to occur between the facilitator and the visitor and among the individual tour participants.

Behind-the-scenes access to these objects through guided tours allows the visitors to see the object devoid of an artificially created environment. When objects are placed on exhibit, curators take great pains to place an item in context, to carefully craft its exhibit label to tell the visitor the who, what, where, and why. Having visitors see the objects in the storeroom permits them to formulate ideas and ask questions without an artificially imposed story line. The museum's collection of ethnographic material from the Pan-American Exposition facilitates dialogue. Each visitor will view the items differently and formulate questions based on their personal experiences. While the tours are led to make each participant feel like it was created just for them or their small group, it does follow a predetermined schedule. Participants tour the museum's storerooms and learn from the artifacts that remain. As primary documents, the artifacts and supplemental ephemera paint a very detailed picture about the role of ethnographic exhibits at the fairs. Larger themes of racial stereotypes, notions of "the other," and what we can learn from the objects are addressed.

The *Exposition Tour* is unique to the facility as it explores the collection through the lens of the Pan-American Exposition. The physical building may postdate the fair, but the Buffalo Society of Natural Sciences, parent organization to the Buffalo Museum of Science, does not.

Through an exploration of the artifacts that remain, tour participants gain a more in-depth and personal understanding of the Pan-American Exposition.

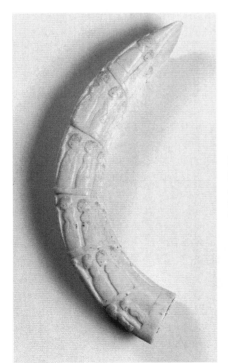

**Figure 8.1. Carved hippopotamus tusk from the African Village at the Pan-American Exposition, Buffalo, 1901. C1512.**
Courtesy of the Buffalo Museum of Science.

The tour begins with a summary of the historical background outlined above and will vary based on the participants' prior knowledge and interests. The key to a good tour is knowing your audience. Since these groups are small, we always begin by asking participants where their interests lie. Why did they sign up for this tour? Are they Pan-American experts? Novices? How familiar are they with the theme? We never want to be repetitive or provide elementary information to a graduate crowd.

Artifacts are introduced, and we employ the inquiry-based learning method made popular by Falk and Dierking.[4] To illustrate this aspect of the tour, we have provided an image of one of the items that is introduced (figure 8.1).

We ask participants: What do you think it is? What do you think it is made from? Does it remind you of anything? Using the participants' answers to move toward the answer keeps the discussion flowing. This particular carved hippopotamus tusk was displayed in the "museum" that was part of the African Village at the Pan-American. A description of the tusk in the promotional brochure from the exposition suggests how it was interpreted in 1901:

> [A] tusk carved with a long procession of women winding round and round spirally from base to tip. It looks like an ordinary piece of native carving, having a purely decorative purpose. As a matter of fact it is a sort of family tree. The carver of this tusk added a new figure every time he took a new wife. The array of women presented in the carving will not seem an extravagant number when it is remembered that Chief Ogolaurie, who is headman of the village has 53 wives at home mourning his absence, only three of his favorites being permitted to accompany him as part of the exhibit.[5]

Polygamy excited Victorian minds by challenging nineteenth-century views on marriage. Linking the object to the life story of a person in the village seemed to validate the object's interpretation, while at the same time "authenticating" the view of African life being presented in Buffalo. But how true was this description? Polygamy was practiced in many West African societies. However, none of the African Villagers, including Chief Ogolaurie, was identified as a polygamist on the passenger lists of the ship that brought them to America. Was Ogolaurie's polygamy hidden from the authorities to make it easier for him to enter the United States? Or was the story of his polygamy created to entice American audiences?

Artifacts showing the multiple facets of village life are shown on the *Exposition Tour*. The "special" pieces, like the tusk illustrated above, would have been in the village's museum. These special artifacts are discussed in relation to the more utilitarian pieces in the collection like undecorated wooden spoons and bowls that villagers would have used while living in Buffalo. The collection also contains examples of recreation: games, toys, and smoking pipes, alluding to the free time available to the performers. These artifacts are laid out for tour participants to view up close. However, since the tour takes place in the storage room, attendees are surrounded by the material culture from the fair. A canoe from the Pan-American hangs overhead while the grass skirts worn by the performers lay in an opened box for closer inspection.

In addition to the artifacts, the Buffalo Museum of Science is fortunate to have a small collection of glass plate negatives of life inside the African Village. Since cameras were a luxury item, unless the official photograph was purchased, personal snapshots were scarce. With the society's commission, the museum was also permitted to photograph the village in order to add to the scientific record. Museum staff member Carlos Cummings documented the African Village for the society.

**Figure 8.2.  Life in the African Village, Pan-American Exposition, Buffalo, 1901.**
Courtesy of the Buffalo Museum of Science.

During the *Exposition Tour*, participants are invited to look at enlarged reproductions of the images, blown up and mounted on a piece of 24 × 36-inch foam core. These images are another way to encourage dialogue and add context to the artifacts in storage. Included is an example of how we encourage participants to read the photographs (figure 8.2).

Look closely at this photograph. What do you see? Do you notice the man behind the tree? Is he lurking? Is the white man invading the individual's privacy? A fair-goer observing a kind of life he's never witnessed before? It can be argued that everyone in this photograph was doing exactly what they were expected to do. Exposition visitors were encouraged to visit, observe, learn, and form their own opinions. Those living in the African Village knew that they were there to be observed. Are we comfortable with this? Does it change your perception of this scene to know that the man standing behind the tree is the photographer, Carlos Cummings, who worked in the village every day for five months and knew all its inhabitants personally?

Look closely at the women as they work. Are you, the observer, now doing anything more sinister than the man behind the tree? Notice their bare feet and then turn your attention to the baby's feet. The mother works in bare feet, as would have been common in Dahomey, but her daughter wears new patent leather shoes that must have been bought in Buffalo. The baby has been identified as Marie, the one-year-old daughter of one of the village's goldsmiths.[6] The goldsmiths received higher wages than other trades and may have been permitted to keep some of the proceeds from their sales. Did he use his income to buy his daughter the newest fashion in shoes? Did he and his wife want her to appear "western" or just protect her feet as she learned to walk?

The chair the woman sits on was one of hundreds provided by the Buffalo Museum of Science for use in the African Village. Carlos Cummings, the man in the background, helped to transport them from the museum to the fair at the request of the villagers.[7] Think about the contrast between the women working with palm-leaf baskets, outdated but still-efficient tools from Africa, and the web of electrical wires overhead, the highest of all high-tech symbols in 1901. Without the presence of the wires, would we know this image was somewhere other than Dahomey? Is it ironic or amazing? What else do you see?

We contrast that with this image (figure 8.3), where Cummings faces the camera alongside an unknown woman from the African Village. Does this pose make us more comfortable? Is there anything to be learned from his body language? The photographs provide another lens into the fair's multifaceted narrative.

Other images from the fair show visitors interacting with the villagers. These images undermine the well-cherished myths about the African Village. The fact that the performers and visitors engaged in conversation makes it

Figure 8.3.   Carlos E. Cummings with an unidentified woman from the African Village at the Pan-American Exposition, Buffalo, 1901.
Courtesy of the Buffalo Museum of Science.

clear that some of the villagers spoke English or French and could interpret their lives directly to the public. They were not captives held in a ghetto-like enclosure, unable to convey their oppression to those who came to see them. From the ease exhibited in their postures, it is also clear that fair-goers did not recoil in horror at the savagery of the men before them. The photographs show men and women from very different cultures connecting as individuals, something that very rarely happened in 1901 without public forums like world's fairs and expositions.

While you could argue that large images could be shown anywhere, the images are just one additional layer to the story. We then explore more of the actual artifacts seen in the photographs. The realization that the participants are standing in front of the skirt that the young man in the photograph is wearing is powerful. The actual object possesses a power that a photograph can never replace. Museologists have argued about the power of the object for decades—is that not why we dedicate so much time to the appropriate care and management of these collections? However, without sharing the artifact's stories, their history, or their narrative, they are no more than inanimate objects on a shelf.

While the *Exposition Tour* was developed with an adult audience in mind, it can certainly be scaled according to participant. At present, behind-the-scenes tours are offered on a monthly basis with required preregistration. We limit the group size to twelve in order to allow for discussion and take into consideration the logistics of the small storage rooms and security of the material. That said, these tours are also available upon request by groups. Alumni associations, service organizations, and senior groups have taken advantage of these offerings. When the participants in the group are known to one another and have a shared interest, it allows for the discussion to change course.

While this program in no way claims to be the progenitor of behind-the-scenes collection tours, it is presented here as a way to organize a previously haphazard occurrence into something meaningful, repeatable, and marketable. In addition, theming the tours allows for repeat visitation. Building on the success of the Pan-American *Exposition Tour*, we have since added a second tour entitled *Knox Your Average Piggy Bank.* This new tour looks at the museum's Knox Money Collection, an assemblage of almost 3,000 artifacts used as money prior to a standardized system of exchange.

Offering behind-the-scenes tours of a museum's collection is certainly nothing revolutionary. This particular program is worthy of note as it provides unexpected historical content in a science museum. The goal was to look at the collection as the backdrop for delivering historical subject matter to allow for contemporary discourse. While public exhibits may need to focus on the core subjects of an institution's mission (in this case, science), a little imagination can open up endless opportunities for behind-the-scenes access. By their very nature, tours are short introductions to a topic, and their fluid nature allows for experimentation. If a line of inquiry does not go according to plan during one tour, it can be changed and redirected during the next iteration. Tours can also be used to garner support and increased interest in a particular collection. This, in turn, could lead to the development of a large-scale exhibition drawing on the feedback from the tours. Museum workers know the costs associated with a permanent exhibit; themed tours do not come with this same permanence, or price tag. After all, science is all about experimentation—who said you can't experiment with history?

## NOTES

1. Xavier Pene, *Darkest Africa; Real African Life in a Real African Village* (Manuscript on file, Buffalo Museum of Science Research Library, 1901).
2. Kevin Smith, *Exhibition Script; Through a Clouded Mirror, Africa at the Pan-American Exposition, Buffalo 1901* (Manuscript on file, Buffalo Museum of Science Research Library, 2001).
3. John Tevi, *A Tour around the World and the Adventures of Dahomey Village [sic]* (Manuscript from the collection of Sonia Tevi-Benissan).
4. John H. Falk and Lynn D. Dierking, *The Museum Experience* (Washington: Whalesback Books, 1992); and John H. Falk and Lynn D. Dierking, *Lessons without Limit: How Free-Choice Learning Is Transforming Education* (New York: AltaMira Press, 2002).
5. Pene, *Darkest Africa*, 11.
6. Smith, *Exhibition Script.*
7. Elizabeth Jane Letson, *Diary* (Manuscript on file, Buffalo Museum of Science Research Library, 1901).

*Chapter Nine*

# "I Cannot Vote, but I Can Be Voted For"

## *A Girl Scout Badge Program*

### Ann Marie Linnabery

*The glory of each generation is to make its own precedents.*

—*Belva Lockwood*

The History Center of Niagara is the umbrella organization for three historic sites in Lockport, New York, operated by the Niagara County Historical Society. These include the main museum complex at 215 Niagara Street, the Erie Canal Discovery Center at 24 Church Street, and the Colonel William Bond/ Jesse Hawley House at 143 Ontario Street. The five-building complex on Niagara Street, opened in 1955, contains exhibits on the county history of the Tuscarora and Seneca Indian Nations, early pioneer settlement, agriculture and trades, the Civil War, transportation, and business and industry. The Erie Canal Discovery Center is an interactive multimedia facility opened in 2005 that interprets the history of the building of the "Flight of Five" Erie Canal Locks at Lockport. The Bond/Hawley House is an 1823 National Register, historic house museum interpreting the late Empire/early Victorian period and its connections to two men involved in the development of the Erie Canal and the village of Lockport. The three sites are tied together by a common theme of the Erie Canal by setting the stage with contextual exhibits; introducing influential personalities; and explaining the challenges of building the locks and the canal, and how this affected local, state, and national history.

Making this rich history accessible and available to large audiences is an issue faced by many cultural institutions. Small-town historical societies and centers often face the added challenge of small budgets, small staff, and a heavy reliance on volunteers. The History Center of Niagara is always striving to share history with a larger and more diverse audience. Collaboration

and partnership is often a key ingredient in the development of new programming, and so began the Belva Lockwood Girl Scout Badge. Not only
did this badge expand the offerings of the history center, it blossomed into
a program to introduce the younger generation to one of Niagara County's
true trailblazers. Though the Scouts expect to encounter history at a historical
society, they are surprised to find such an inspiring person who lived in their
own "backyard."

Belva Ann Bennett was born in a log cabin in Royalton, New York, on
October 24, 1830, to a poor farming family. At age 18, she married a local
farmer, Uriah McNall, and had a daughter named Lura. After her husband
died three years later, Belva McNall realized she had to earn a living on her
own, so she taught school and took classes to further her education. In 1854,
she enrolled in the Genesee Wesleyan College in Lima, New York. She met
women's rights activists and took an interest in law. In 1857, Belva was hired
as the preceptress of the girls' department at the Lockport Union School at
half the salary of the male teachers. Four years later, she left Lockport to ad-
minister and teach at two female seminaries in western New York. She soon
grew restless however, and longed to try a new vocation: the law.

In 1866, Belva McNall set off for Washington, DC, to establish a new
school called McNall's Female Seminary and embarked on a new career.
Two years later, she married Ezekiel Lockwood, a dentist, and had another
daughter who died in infancy. That same year, National University began
accepting women into their law school. Lockwood and another woman completed their degrees in 1873 but were denied their diplomas on the basis of
their sex. Lockwood wrote directly to US President Ulysses Grant to demand
her diploma. Two weeks later, she received the diploma. While Lockwood
was now admitted to the DC bar, there were other hurdles she encountered.
After a five-year battle with Congress, on February 7, 1879, the US Senate
voted thirty-nine to twenty allowing women the right to argue cases in the
highest court in the land, the US Supreme Court.

With this battle won, Belva Lockwood again grew restless and wanted to
do more for women's rights. In August 1884, Lockwood was nominated for
the office of President of the United States at the Woman's National Equal
Rights Party Convention. She readily accepted and adopted a platform addressing twelve important issues of the day. She relished the campaign, but
newspaper editorials and cartoons derided her nomination. On Election Day,
Belva Lockwood received just over 4,000 votes, the first woman to receive
votes in a national election. Grover Cleveland, of Buffalo, won the election. Four years later, Lockwood ran again but received even fewer votes.
Lockwood continued her law practice and became involved in the Universal
Peace Union. The highlight of Belva Lockwood's legal career occurred in

1905 when, after thirty years of effort, she was part of a legal team that won a five-million-dollar settlement for the Cherokee Indians against the US government. Her final years were passed in her law practice, working for world peace and supporting women's suffrage. She died on May 20, 1917, and is buried in Congressional Cemetery in Washington, DC.

The Girl Scouts have been using badges to honor accomplishments since the organization was founded in 1912. Badges are earned when a Scout completes a series of requirements that are related to a particular activity. The official Girl Scout website describes the importance of badges as a cornerstone of Girl Scouting. There are seven legacy badges that build on more than a hundred years of Girl Scout history. Each of these badges (Artist, Athlete, Citizen, Cook, First Aid, Girl Scout Way, and Naturalist) is available at five levels of Girl Scouting.[1] In addition to the legacy badges, there are a plethora of other badges that can be earned, and each council has their own badges unique to their area. The Girl Scouts of Western New York offer seventeen of their own badges, most of which focus on local history.[2]

The Belva Lockwood Girl Scout Badge was created in anticipation of the nation's bicentennial in 1976. Each Girl Scout council was asked to honor two women in their region who had made a difference in either local or national history. One of the women chosen by the Niagara County Girl Scout Council was Belva Lockwood. According to one source, three Royalton, New York, Girl Scouts—Roselee Sworts, Stephanie LePard, and Holly Ortman—created a special badge to honor the most famous woman from their town. The first badges were handmade by Mrs. Pearl Schumacher. On November 23, 1975, a special ceremony was held to dedicate a plaque on Griswold Road in Royalton commemorating the birthplace of Belva Lockwood.[3] The badge remained a local achievement for the "Belvadears," local troops from the towns of Gasport, Middleport, and Barker until Edna Stubbs, Program Director for the Niagara Council, decided "we had to do something [council-wide] about Belva Lockwood."[4] In the early 1980s, in response to the US Postal Service's "Great Americans" series, the Niagara County Girl Scout Council nominated Belva Lockwood to be honored with a stamp. It was at this point that the council began promoting a badge to honor Belva Lockwood to troops throughout Niagara County. At first, it was only offered to Junior Girl Scouts, but over the next several years, Brownies, then Cadets, and finally Seniors were eligible to earn the badge.[5]

With the regional and age-level expansion of the badge, Niagara County Girl Scouts Program Director Edna Stubbs collaborated with the Niagara County Historical Society to create a more structured program, known as the *Belva Lockwood Badge*, with specific requirements for girls to receive their badge.[6] This partnership gave the Girl Scouts a starting point for working on the badge. Some of the activities associated with the badge are reflected in the themes of the history center's exhibits, which examine local people, places, and times and connect them to issues and events of a larger, national significance. One purpose of the *Belva Lockwood Badge* was to introduce local Girl Scouts to this Niagara County woman who defied the restrictions that society had placed on females in the nineteenth century and demonstrated that women could not only navigate, but also succeed, on their own in a man's world. Although Belva Lockwood's big moment in history had occurred in the 1880s, the timing of the program was ideal considering the political and social advances women were making a hundred years later.

The 1980s could be viewed as a series of watershed moments for women's achievements in US history. In 1981, just over a hundred years after Belva Lockwood became the first woman to try a case in the US Supreme Court, Sandra Day O'Connor became the first female justice appointed to serve on that federal judicial body. Three years later, exactly a hundred years after Belva's run for the presidency, Geraldine Ferraro became the first woman to be chosen as a vice presidential running mate on a major party ticket with Democratic presidential candidate Walter Mondale. Almost mirroring Belva Lockwood's life, Sandra Day O'Connor had a long and successful tenure at the Supreme Court, while Geraldine Ferraro lost her bid for the vice presidency. Like Belva had done a hundred years earlier, both of these women pushed the limits of their gender and opened doors for future generations. Ignoring the boundaries that dictated what men could do but women couldn't was something Belva Lockwood had aspired to all her life and ultimately something in which she succeeded.

So how did it happen that Belva Lockwood became a mentor for Girl Scouts in western New York even though her greatest achievements occurred when she was living in Washington, DC? A Girl Scout leader, whose troop participated in the badge program, remarked that Belva Lockwood and Juliette Gordon Low, founder of the Girl Guides (later changed to Girl Scouts), both emphasized the importance of self-sufficiency and self-confidence in girls and women and both were criticized for their promotion of what were, at that time, unladylike activities and views.[7] The Girl Scouts were started by Low in 1912 and modeled after the Girl Guide movement in England.[8] Originally open to girls ages ten to eighteen, it was later expanded to include younger girls. Today there are five levels of Girl Scouts: Daisies (kindergarten to first grade), Brownies (second to third grade), Juniors (fourth to fifth grade), Cadettes (sixth to eighth grade), and Seniors (ninth to tenth grade), and Ambassadors (eleventh to twelfth grade). The organization emphasizes leadership skills, self-confidence, friendship, and citizenship through a variety of activities including group meetings, special events, camping, and community involvement. Today there are 1.7 million Girl Scouts and 750,000 adult volunteers working in more than one hundred councils across the United States. There are also Girl Scout councils in ninety-two countries worldwide.[9]

As mentioned in the introduction, this badge program was initially created in 1975 by three local Girl Scouts specifically for their own troop. Since then, troops at all age levels have participated and come from urban, rural, and suburban areas not only in Niagara County but also from the neighboring counties as well. The topic of gender equality transcends geographic areas, but many of the resources and the physical connections to Belva Lockwood are unique to Niagara County and are available at the history center.

The Girl Scouts who participate in this program, even those who live nearby, usually come with little or no knowledge of who Belva Lockwood was or what she did to earn her place in history. Depending on the age of the girls, some come in expecting to hear about some old, dead woman who has little impact and no relation to their lives today, only to learn that they actually do have some common ground with her as well as some very different experiences. The two-hour program starts with a brief thirty-minute introduction to Belva Lockwood's life and career through a PowerPoint presentation. Rather than just giving a narrative of her life, we discuss the similarities and differences between her childhood and theirs. As the dialogue moves forward, there is a question/answer conversation about the opportunities and the restrictions Lockwood and other women encountered in the nineteenth century and how those have changed or stayed the same over time. Some of the questions asked include these: How would you feel if your father said, "if only you had been a boy"? How would you feel if you found out your brother was paid more than you for doing the same chore? What would you do if you were not allowed to graduate from school just because you were a girl? Do you think there are any positive aspects to being a woman in the nineteenth century? We explain that, believe it or not, some women were actually glad their husbands earned the money in the family and they did not have to work outside the home or involve themselves in politics or economics. The objective of this part of the program is to get the girls to consider the fact that women have not always had the freedom and options that are available now and that there were women who lived before them who broke down the barriers and paved the way for them.

As the program moves into events that took place later in Lockwood's life, the participants begin to realize how events that took place 150 years ago actually do have an impact on their lives today. For example, we point out that something as common as a woman riding a bicycle today was considered immodest and scandalous in the 1880s. Belva Lockwood, however, ignored the naysayers and used a three-wheeled bicycle to get around Washington, DC.[10]

We then ask them questions such as: Do you think she was criticized and mocked? Did she acknowledge these comments and abandon her bicycle? What if she had given in to her detractors? Would other women have been reluctant to ride bicycles? How many years, or even decades, would have passed before it was acceptable for women to ride bicycles? Would you be allowed to ride a bicycle today if it had not been for courageous women like Belva Lockwood? Another example involves ladies' fashions. The clothing Belva Lockwood was expected to wear was uncomfortable and restrictive. We ask the girls why they think this was so and if some women had not defied the custom of wearing a corset, or had not been brave enough to start wearing bloomers (women's pantaloons) under their dresses, might women today still be suffering the effects of a restricting undergarment or the physical limitations of a cumbersome dress? These are things that women today take for granted but something our sisters 150 years ago struggled with every day. This is one of the considerations we want the girls to come away with when they complete the program.

In addition to examining Belva Lockwood's life and how she influenced the lives of women today, the program also includes a brief thirty-minute tour of a few of the history center's exhibits that have an association with her experiences in Niagara County. This offers a tangible link to the past and allows the Scouts to make a connection with the people and the places that were previously discussed. These areas include the Pioneer Cabin, to illustrate the type of environment Lockwood was born into; the Barn, which contains agricultural exhibits as well as the original Lockport Union School bell; and the Washington Hunt Law Office, where there is a portrait of Belva Lockwood and a set of china that she owned.

Following the tour, the Scouts reconvene in the history center meeting room to complete one or more additional topics. When the badge program was first developed for just Junior Girl Scouts, six activities out of a possible nine were required. To paraphrase, the nine options were to visit the Belva Lockwood Memorial on Griswold Road in Royalton; list ten facts about her life; read one of two juvenile biographies of her life or write a 200-word report on an event in her life; visit the Niagara County Historical Society; explain what Lockwood meant by her statement, "I never lose. I set a precedent, and every time a woman sets a precedent, she wins a victory";[11] make a campaign poster Lockwood might have used in 1884 or 1888; explain the meaning of the words "temperance" and "women's suffrage"; learn what life was like for women in the 1840s and 1850s and why Lockwood objected to it; and support the movement to have the US Postal Service issue a stamp to honor Belva Lockwood (this option was dropped after the stamp was issued in 1986).

**Figure 9.1.    Girl Scouts look at the portrait of Belva Lockwood.**
Courtesy of the History Center of Niagara.

When the program was expanded to include other age groups, eight additional options were added to the requirements. Brownies need to complete four of the total activites, Juniors six, Cadets eight, and Seniors and Ambassadors ten. The new selections included visiting a one-room schoolhouse; "meeting" Belva Lockwood portrayed by a costumed interpreter; writing and presenting a five-minute speech about a topic that was important to Lockwood; learning the "Dear Belva" song; organizing and/or participating in an event for Women's History Month in March; learning about careers in the law profession; and reading a biography of a woman who was a contemporary of Belva Lockwood and who was also a trailblazer in women's history; view facsimiles of Lockwood's campaign ephemera and design a set of materials she might use if she were running for president today. It is up to the troop leader as to which requirements they want to do. Many can be done at the troop meeting.

Regardless of age level, the most requested activities to do at the history center are the campaign poster and the discussion of what life was like for women in the 1840s and 1850s and why Belva Lockwood rebelled against it. A few leaders want the Scouts to read one of the books about Belva Lockwood available at the history center. In lieu of visiting a one-room schoolhouse, some troops opt to use the history center's One-Room School House

Teaching Box (either at the history center or at their own meeting) to learn
and do hands-on activities related to that topic. These include writing with a
quill pen, using a horn book, playing games with chalk and a slate, studying
simple lessons from the 1860s, discussing what students ate for lunch, and
learning the rules for students (and teachers too). Each of these activities take
an additional thirty minutes to complete, bringing the program to two hours.

During the course of the program, the Scouts view and use primary sources
while touring the exhibits and doing the activities. For example, while touring
the history center, the Scouts see and learn about how a nineteenth-century
laptop desk was used during the era when Belva McNall would have been
teaching school. In the Pioneer Cabin and Barn, they view objects associated
with chores that children would have done when Lockwood was a child. We
also use reproductions of original photographs, campaign materials, political cartoons, letters, newspapers, and other documents as primary sources.
There are two documents from Lockwood's 1884 campaign that are utilized
in making the posters. One is an image of Lockwood that was used in newspapers and other publicity; the other is a handbill announcing Lockwood and
Marietta Stow (vice presidential candidate) as the Equal Rights Party ticket.
Two political cartoons from 1884 are displayed to demonstrate the negative
attitude many people had toward Lockwood and her bid for the presidency.
Other documents include a letter describing her time as preceptress at the
Union School in Lockport, a Christmas card, and a postcard relating to the
death of her daughter. All are written and signed "Belva Lockwood." Numer-
ous photographs from Lockwood's life, and of Lockport during her years

Figure 9.2.    Voting ballot for the presidential election of 1884. Unknown artist. Printing on paper. Collection of Oakland Museum of California. Gift of Gertrude Smyth.
Courtesy of the Oakland Museum of California.

here, are also exhibited. These materials demonstrate how historical documents, as well as events, can still have relevance today.

Although the *Belva Lockwood Badge* program attracts two to three troops a year, the geographic area of where those troops come from is widening, with some traveling one to two hours to visit the history center and the other Lockwood associated sites in Niagara County. Also, over the years, as staff and volunteers change, the program has evolved as each facilitator brings his or her own knowledge and personal touch to the activities done at the history center. Although the facts about Lockwood's life do not change, how they are presented and how activities are conducted have changed over time with different facilitators building on and bringing something new to the program.

In the last decade, the *Belva Lockwood Badge* has also been adapted for use as an outreach program in the classroom or can be conducted during a field trip to the history center. In 2008, when Barack Obama and Hillary Clinton were campaigning for the presidency, there was increased interest in learning about other presidential candidates who broke barriers to compete for that office. An activity was developed specifically for grades one through three that introduced them to women and people of color who had previously run for president, albeit unsuccessfully, but who had not let discrimination or negative attitudes hold them back. Because of her local connection, Belva Lockwood was discussed at more length than the others. The program ended with the students voting in an election to decide the favorite food in the class by casting paper ballots in an antique ballot box. This program was further modified for grades four through seven by exchanging the voting activity for a lesson about the history of voting rights from 1790 to the present and having them place each voting rights law in chronological order. For grades eight through twelve, the activity is a document-based question having them analyze political cartoons from Belva Lockwood's campaign. The discussion of the presidential candidates who broke barriers is retained at all three levels, but the information given increases in length and complexity as the grades advance. With the right approach, the program could be adapted for use as a Boy Scout badge also.

One of the most rewarding aspects of the *Belva Lockwood Badge* has been watching the evolution of the Scouts' interest and awareness as they learn more about this undaunted woman who lived and worked within close proximity to where they themselves are growing up and going to school. They are shocked to discover how many restrictions were placed upon women in the nineteenth century and slowly begin to understand (and empathize with) the plight of their female ancestors. When you see them suddenly recognize, "Hey, this could have been me if I had lived 150 years ago," you know that the objective of the program has been realized and your efforts have succeeded. One Scout summed it up this way: "It is interesting to see how Belva Lockwood's courage and leadership not only shaped our nation's history but also how she transformed the way people view women's roles in society and politics."[12]

## NOTES

1. "Traditions," Girl Scouts, https://www.girlscouts.org/en/about-girl-scouts/traditions.html.

2. "Badges," Girl Scouts of Western New York, https://www.gswny.org/en/our-program/badges.html.

3. "Girl Scouts Carry on Belva's Legacy," Middleport, New York, August 14, 2017, http://middleport-newyork.com/girl-scouts-carry-belvas-legacy/.

4. Edna Stubbs, telephone interview with author, July 8, 2019.

5. Stubbs.

6. Stubbs.

7. Karen Spiegel, Girl Scout Leader, telephone interview with author, July 15, 2019.

8. "Juliette Gordon Low," Girl Scouts, https://www.girlscouts.org/en/about-girl-scouts/our-history/juliette-gordon-low.html.

9. "Who We Are," Girl Scouts, https://www.girlscouts.org/en/about-girl-scouts/who-we-are.html.

10. Jill Norgren, *Belva Lockwood: The Woman Who Would Be President* (London: New York, 2008).

11. Guidelines for WNY *Belva Lockwood Badge*, Girl Scouts of Western New York (original 1986; revised 2011), https://www.gswny.org/content/dam/girlscouts-gswny/documents/co-Belva_Lockwood.pdf.

12. Girl Scout from Karen Spiegel's Troop following May 11, 2019, *Belva Lockwood Badge* program.

*Chapter Ten*

# At Rest in the Weeds

## The Restoration of Institutional Cemeteries

David Mack-Hardiman

*There was a common question asked of me about ghosts. I responded that in my days in the cemeteries, the only things that I'd seen were beautiful animals; a red fox, hawks, a newborn fawn, woodpeckers, snakes and ground hogs. And, the only spirit that I'd felt was one of community for these diverse groups coming together to bring dignity to these long abandoned wards of the state.*

—*David Mack-Hardiman*

For twenty years, the Museum of disABILITY History has stood alone as the only brick-and-mortar facility of its kind, dedicated exclusively to preserving the history of people who have disabling conditions, their struggles, their successes, and their impact on American society. Presented with balanced perspectives, the exhibits, programs, and publications place the history of people who have disabilities in context, while striving to change attitudes and perceptions. While creating platforms for dialogue and discovery, the museum seeks a higher level of societal awareness to advance the understanding, acceptance, and independence of people who have disabilities. Located outside of Buffalo in the Town of Amherst, New York, the museum has received national and international visitors, attention, and publicity. One of its recent programs, *Cemetery Restoration*, has been instrumental in increasing the profile of the museum, its mission, and its role in changing the perception of people with disabling conditions.

Seemingly abandoned cemeteries can be found throughout the United States. Each stone-marked plot may be all that remains of a life once lived. While the focus of the Museum of disABILITY History's cemetery projects have focused on a specific population, their methods, advocacy, and outcomes can be used to teach about past populations from various communities.

**Figure 10.1.  Markers are broken, unreadable, and have fallen victim to the elements.**
Courtesy of the Museum of disABILITY History.

Many people in this country are completely unaware of a very dark aspect of American history, as it has been cloaked in a shroud of secluded mystery. Snared in the web of the eugenics movement, thousands of Americans were sent to live in massive institutions. The culture of eugenics supported the segregation of those viewed as needy or less desirable. Once confined to these remote facilities, some were surgically sterilized so that their "disability" would not be passed on to further generations. New immigrants were especially vulnerable to being sequestered in these institutions.

At various times, thousands of people lived and worked in these cloistered settlements, tucked away in rural areas in western New York. Here we discuss just three of the myriad facilities used to remove these people from their families and communities. One was a homeopathic hospital and later psychiatric center located in a valley in northern Cattaraugus County next to the Seneca Nation. Another was a colony that served people who had epilepsy in the tiny hamlet of Sonyea in Livingston County, sixty-five miles east of Buffalo, New York. And in Niagara County to the north of Erie County, an almshouse was home to people in need in the Town of Lockport. Hidden away at the far reaches of the institutional properties, these abandoned graveyards have been the focus of the Museum of disABILITY History *Cemetery Restoration* project for thirteen years. Institutional structures have been repurposed or abandoned. Some have been spruced up as correctional facilities. The remains of those people who lived in these buildings were relegated to the graveyards that are untouched. Yet, to truly feel the utter depersonalization and isolation of these institutional environments, a visit to the cemeteries is the only remaining glimpse. Rows of numbered markers, illegible or broken, are tossed into a mire of weeds and ivy.

Humans have been burying their dead for thousands of years, for a variety of reasons, including superstition, religious beliefs, public health concerns, a sense of closure for family or loved ones, and out of reverence or respect. In the United States, there are thousands of cemeteries scattered throughout the land. The wealthy dead are remembered with huge granite mausoleums, towering obelisks, carefully carved statues, and poetic epitaphs. Watched by angels or guarded by gargoyles, those of money who have gone before rest in cemeteries of breathtaking beauty. Every variety of tree, shrub, and flower imaginable inhabit the more exclusive resting places with exquisite granite fainting couches for mourning or musing. Grounds are manicured with meticulous precision. But for people who were confined to these institutions, their final resting places were not nearly as elaborate.

The *Cemetery Restoration* program was designed to bring awareness to disability history. At its beginning, the museum joined a statewide alliance known as the 1033 Group. Through conference calls and email communication with the group, abandoned cemeteries were identified that needed attention. The *Cemetery Restoration* team was formed and consisted of volunteers who were interested in improving the current condition of these abandoned cemeteries. To learn about proper techniques to use during the restoration work, the Western New York Association of Historical Agencies sponsored the workshop *Grave Matters.* Through the workshop, volunteers learned about the appropriate cleaning supplies to use like soft bristle brushes, as well as ways to reset table markers so as not to damage the stones. Before the start of each restoration project, the volunteers also met the superintendents of the respective facilities and found they were generous in their support and assistance. For each *Cemetery Restoration* project, a van was utilized to carry supplies for the volunteers. This included small plastic stools, brushes of all sizes, spray bottles, water buckets, a large folding table, insect repellent, gloves, a first aid kit, and hand sanitizer. Additionally, a cooler contained water, snacks, and lunch items.

One of the first restoration sites was located in Gowanda, New York, a sleepy town just south of the Erie County line. This valley surrounded by hills is the former home of the large Homeopathic State Hospital, which opened in 1896 and later became a psychiatric center. There were two cemeteries that served the facility. The older one is located off Wheater Road and the newer one is on Route 62. In total, there are more than 1,700 graves. The original cemetery is nestled in a hollow along the banks of Clear Creek. Upon arrival, one is struck by the harshness of the rust-colored cast-iron numbers, which are the singular remembrance of patients buried in the front sections. In another section, there are upright stones with numbers and religious symbols. In yet another area, beyond a dilapidated gate, there are small square markers that lie flat on the ground. Just numbers, *sine nomine.*

The *Cemetery Restoration* team for these two Gowanda sites was a collaborative effort and varied from week to week. The project relied on partnerships, but the most loyal volunteers were from the Cattaraugus County Mental Health Association, employees of People Inc. and the Museum of disABILITY History, college students from St. Bonaventure University and Siena College, and students from the Randolph Children's Home. Originally, Randolph Children's Home was an orphanage for children left parentless by the Civil War and today it is the residential campus for children who are judged to be "at risk." Before beginning the restoration, each group received a brief orientation to the graveyard and a demonstration of available work projects.

At the Route 62 site, every grave was recorded. Each one was photographed and described in detail. Some had tiny nameplates and others did not. Volunteers sat in the grass and wrote about the legibility of the number and the condition of the religious emblem. It was noticed that the numbering sequence had some gaps, which became the first mystery. One young intern displayed refreshing perseverance in trying to find the missing stones. Some had dropped beneath grass level and were obscured by the regrowth. Whenever a number was missing, the volunteer did not rest until it was located, unearthed, and back in its rightful place. Even the young children from the Randolph Children's Home helped out. They were especially excited whenever they unearthed a missing headstone and could clean and return it to where it could now be seen. Another intern made a huge map, noting the number, religion, and location of every single grave. All of this information has been extremely helpful for families searching for ancestral graves.

In the older cemetery on Wheater Road, the task was a little more daunting and took three summers to complete. The most time-consuming aspect was unearthing 550 buried headstones, which was done successfully by diligent and dedicated volunteers. First, they would guess where the next grave should be based on spacing estimates. Next, they tapped the ground to determine resistance. A larger square of sod was cut from the top, and then the stones were pulled to safety. After being given a water bath, the headstones were put back on top of the earth where they had been found. The group spent a total of four summers in the Gowanda graveyards, and work continues to assist families who want to visit today. In addition, monuments have been installed, flower beds planted, and new signage created.

Another *Cemetery Restoration* program was in Sonyea, next to Keshequa Creek Gorge, at the location of the Craig Colony for Epileptics. The original colony, founded in 1894, had cottages for women named for flowers and those for men named for trees. In a remote graveyard on Moyer Road, more than 2,000 colony patients are buried. These graves had been previously photographed and posted to a cemetery website. For this project, the museum personnel were joined by loyal volunteers, which included friends from the Self-Advocacy Association of the Finger Lakes area. Small white stones displaying the names of the deceased had fallen victim to lawn-mower vibrations and the cruelty of time. The headstones were a greenish-gray color as they were encrusted with lichen and fungus. Large religious statues and fragrant lilac trees did little to temper the stark reality of the tiny broken stones.

**Figure 10.2. Gravestone at the Craig Colony Cemetery on Moyer Road in Sonyea, New York, before cleaning.**
Courtesy of Christopher and Tara Schrull.

**Figure 10.3. Once the volunteers were finished, the names of the deceased were once again visible, as seen here in a gravestone from the Craig Colony Cemetery in Sonyea, New York.**
Courtesy of Christopher and Tara Schrull.

The volunteers sat on folding stools and sprayed and scrubbed the stones until slowly the names took shape. Each stone took up to one half hour to clean. In hushed tones, the volunteers often discussed the names they had uncovered, audibly musing about who that person may have been. Deeper within the Sonyea Forest is an older cemetery with cast-iron numbers, similar to those seen in Gowanda. For two summers, the *Cemetery Restoration* team dedicated its time to cleaning stones so the identities or burial places could be seen.

On Poor House Hill in Lockport, across from the current Niagara County Jail, there is a cemetery with 1,400 burials of residents from the first almshouse in the county. Such facilities served many types of people who required social support including unwed mothers, people who simply had no money, and people who had various diseases, head trauma, or mental illness. While the almshouse structure is gone, there is a crumbling silo still standing at the edge of the path on the hill. The members of the Niagara County Historian's Office assisted the *Cemetery Restoration* team by sharing their records of those interred there. The Niagara County Sheriff's Office and the Parks and Grounds Department also offered practical assistance. Additional help came from a group of employees from the Western New York Developmental Disabilities State Operation and Offices.

Nature had grown a protective covering over the long-neglected Niagara County Almshouse Cemetery that had burials recorded from 1830 to 1912.

Serpentine grapevines wound around the trees and grew horizontally, making it nearly impenetrable. Poison ivy hid among the weeds, cleverly blending in with the surrounding vegetation. Sturdy canvas gloves and sharpened garden shears were mandatory in this remote graveyard because thorns hid everywhere. Unfortunate helpers attracted sticky clumps of burdock that took extensive grooming sessions to extract. There appeared to be only one family gravestone, cracked and falling apart. Stone Art Memorial Company took on the challenge of restoring this headstone, adding a new base and somehow getting it back up the rutted hill. The ambitious volunteers decided to create a memorial garden and with rakes and shovels carved a pathway. Rocks were added to showcase the hardy vinca vine near an ancient apple tree. The Orleans Monument Company donated a beautiful inscribed bench. What once was a symbol of neglect was reborn with the dedication of the loyal workers and the partnerships they forged. The *Cemetery Restoration* team has returned to this cemetery for the past six years to keep the vegetation at bay and preserve this final resting ground.

It is indeed ironic that so little is known about the people who were the subject of such extensive daily documentation. When families make inquiries, there are often reports of fires, floods, or unlucky file transfers in which all documentary evidence was lost. It is unknown where records are kept for institutions that have closed permanently. Sometimes, families are sent from office to office and give up in frustration. Through diligent detective work, relatives are sometimes able to get information. For example, if a date of death is known through obituaries or genealogy websites, descendants can request a copy of the death record through the town clerk in which the facility was located. Sometimes, these documents include information about the person's history at the hospital, their religion, and their ancestry. And, quite amazingly, some of the certificates will make reference to the specific grave number. In Gowanda, there were three distinct religious symbols used. A wreath represented people who were Protestant, a cross was the sign for Catholics, and the Star of David symbolized people who were Jewish. By matching the number and religion to their ancestor, families could finally locate where their ancestors are at rest.

Due in large part to the Museum of disABILITY History *Cemetery Restoration* program, families long separated by imposed segregation can now reunite. One family member from Texas whose ancestor lived in the Gowanda institution shared what it meant to finally find his grandfather's gravesite:

> What can I say about the help that you provided for my family? You have given us our Grandfather. We never met him as the family kept his life a secret to all us children. When I reached out to you, you were able to find his location of burial and we were able to obtain his death certificate. My life changed forever.

Thank you so much for giving me a small part of his life. Growing up we were told that he has passed on in the 1940's. Modern technology and your help have changed that narrative.

The *Cemetery Restoration* program sponsored by the Museum of dis-ABILITY History has received numerous accolades. In June 2014 at the Almshouse Cemetery Restoration Ceremony, the Niagara County Legislature conveyed honorary recognition to the group: "The Museum of disABILITY History, a project of People Inc., is to be congratulated and commended for this outstanding project and the unveiling of a new memorial plaque and restored, permanent monument." Also, in January 2017, the National Federation for Just Communities of Western New York presented the Museum of disABILITY History with the Community Leader Award in Arts and Culture.

The *Cemetery Restoration* program was featured in the 2014 exhibit *Monument for the Forgotten* at the Museum of disABILITY History. The exhibit chronicled the restoration work of the program, and included in it were donated grave markers from some of the institutional cemeteries. For the exhibit, local artist Brian Nesline of *Faces of Buffalo Community Art Mosaics* unveiled his poignant mosaic tapestry work that included hundreds of photographs taken by museum volunteers of individual grave markers, which were woven into an image of a large stone monument. Nesline was very moved as he created his artistic design:

> The exhibit has caused me to face fears, to suspend judgement and to dig deep into my mindful heart in my relations with others and draw upon that loving power whose variety of expression is our common life. I now think of those who were once forgotten as falling stars, who, lost for a season, may rise again as the light of upward momentum for the betterment of all human services. I imagine the written records of the past will be recovered to reveal their names so that going forward, they are always remembered. I admire the volunteers and staff who have and will take action on important initiatives such as this in hopes that identity, both individual and collective, will remain at the forefront of our ever expanding consciousness, never again to be forgotten.[1]

There is so much history down these rural back roads—the history of an entire American movement to cull ordinary citizens and separate them from society, as well as the histories of the institutions themselves and the archaic treatment practices that occurred there. But most importantly, there are the unknown stories of people, buried unceremoniously in anonymous graves. Illustrated here are just three sites in western New York. This is a program to engage citizens in the preservation of local history and to learn the identities of those interred in a community. It is a way to learn through community service, restoration, and caretaking. It is also a call to action to shed light on an underrepresented population in our history. The Museum of disABILITY History's *Cemetery Restoration* program strives to educate the living and help bring dignity to these unnamed dead through the restoration and upkeep of these once lost final resting places.

## NOTE

1. Brian Nesline, Museum of disABILITY History *Newsletter*, Summer edition, 2014.

*Chapter Eleven*

# Windows to History

## *Frank Lloyd Wright's Martin House Light Screens*

### Gina Miano

Frank Lloyd Wright (1867–1959) designed a unique residential complex for wealthy Buffalo, New York, businessman Darwin D. Martin and his family between 1903–1905. The complex consists of six interconnected buildings designed as a unified composition, including the main Martin House and a pergola that connects it to a conservatory and carriage house with chauffeur's quarters and stables, the Barton House, a smaller residence for Martin's sister and brother-in-law, and a gardener's cottage added in 1909. The landscape design for the grounds of the complex is highly integrated with the overall composition of buildings. The most substantial and highly developed of Frank Lloyd Wright's Prairie houses in the eastern United States, the Darwin D. Martin House received National Historic Landmark status in 1986. The house is considered by leading Frank Lloyd Wright scholars as one of Wright's finest achievements of the Prairie period and, indeed, of his entire career.[1]

Over the decades, the Martin House Complex suffered considerable damage, and three of the original five buildings were demolished. In 1992, the Martin House Restoration Corporation was formed to raise funds for and oversee a complete restoration of the complex. Over the past twenty-seven years, there has been considerable restoration, finally completing the restoration and rebuilding of the missing buildings, acquiring furniture and art glass, and starting the planting of the historic landscape.

Traditional historic house museums have multiple narratives on which to build their interpretative tours. Exploring history through the eyes of past inhabitants is often the most common route. The Darwin D. Martin House Complex looks to explore history from diverse perspectives. The resulting program, *Art Glass at the Martin House*, marries traditional narratives, art, architecture, technology, and aesthetics into a comprehensive program that delivers historical content in an unexpected way.

There are many areas of educational interest at the Martin House, one of the strongest being the extensive art glass. There are almost four hundred art glass windows on the complex, each building having their own unique art glass design. Wright called these "light screens" and employed a glass art look, made popular at the time by Louis Comfort Tiffany but in a distinctive, "Wrightian" way.

Visitors to the Martin House are generally interested in the art glass windows because they are so numerous, and they are an important and necessary element to the beauty of the design on the site. It is a tangible, art-focused aspect of architecture that helps the participant to understand geometric design within the larger scope of the house and landscape. There is also a lot of scholarly, historical information available on Frank Lloyd Wright windows. In addition to the many examples of art glass in our possession, we also have many drawings, letters, and primary source documents that show the development and implementation of the different designs. The public interest in the Martin House windows has a long history. The first exhibit was at the Burchfield Penney Art Center in 1999, which showcased the different patterns of the light screens from the Martin House.[2] The goal of the exhibit was to garner interest in the fledgling restoration project. The exhibition was so successful that we realized art glass as an artistic concept was relevant and held the public's interest. The uniqueness of the designs has given us a great opportunity to develop programming built on the history and process of designing art glass, focusing on Wright's desire to be different and how he pushed the limits of what was considered "normal" design.

Building on the interest and importance of art glass, we designed a universal program entitled *Art Glass at the Martin House.* The strength of this program is that it can be tailored to meet a range of grade and age levels. For the purpose of this chapter, I will focus on our on-site field trip program for students eight to twelve years of age. The main goals for this program are for students to understand the history of the Darwin D. Martin House, the family that lived there, Buffalo at the turn of the last century, and how the site is considered to be a significant piece of architecture in the city. This program also focuses on the overall history of art glass windows and the process of art glass making. We want students to understand how natural, organic designs can be formed into geometric abstractions, and how this fit Frank Lloyd Wright's narrative of using nature as his muse to create unique designs. One major educational aspect of this program is in the creativity and production of an artistic piece. We want students to create their own art glass design as an indication of how much they understand the organic to geometric process that Wright utilized.

**Figure 11.1.  Students creating their window designs.**
Collection Martin House, Buffalo, New York.

When a group arrives to the Martin House for the *Art Glass at the Martin House* program, they are shown an introductory film and are then taken on a tour of the site. The trained docents use an inquiry-based learning approach while giving the tour and focus their content to the age of the group. On the tour, students are introduced to historical context of the house. For example, the Martin family was the first in the neighborhood to live in a house designed for electricity, they had a horse and carriage as their main source of transportation, and they used numerous iceboxes to keep their food cold. In addition to hearing about the Martin family history, students learn about Frank Lloyd Wright and various architectural elements featured in the house. The group is given ample time to explore the art glass window designs in various rooms. Students are encouraged to look at the geometric shapes and see beyond them to the organic shapes that they symbolize. Seeing how the organic shapes manifest in the geometric form of the light screens is a key concept to designing their own window as part of the program.

After the initial tour, the group goes to the Junior League Buffalo News Education Center located in the lower level of the Martin House. We created a PowerPoint presentation that shows examples of the Martin House windows alongside more traditional art glass windows like those designed by Louis

Comfort Tiffany[3] and others that we might expect to find in houses of the turn of the last century, or in churches from a similar time period.[4] Through a facilitated dialogue, we lead a discussion on windows. We show that, like other art forms, art glass windows tell a story. We show Wright windows that contrast with the traditional ideas of looking "through windows" to looking "at windows." Through these images, we illustrate how traditional art glass designs were created to be a true depiction of something in life. Many examples are found in churches that show scenes from the Bible. Others, like those we find in houses in Buffalo, show scenes from nature.

In order to provide a hands-on component of the program, we have amassed a collection of the elements used in window design and manufacture that the students can interact with. To illustrate the fragile nature of the elaborate design, we have materials like lead and brass caming, a bracing bar, and different examples of art glass pieces that can be handled. We discuss how artists had to use long bracing bars that cross over the design in order to keep it together. The black caming that frames the pieces of art glass is made of lead came. Lead came, while malleable and easily movable around curves and organic shapes, are also more likely to bend after several years and can easily warp.[5] Conversely, Frank Lloyd Wright used brass came. Brass is not malleable, but when used with geometric shapes like those in the Wright windows this feature was not necessary. This removed the need for a bracing bar, and the windows were not in danger of warping over time.

We then provide the students with images of things that appear in nature and illustrate how they were used to create the geometric shapes in the Wright windows. For example, we show a potted plant and compare it with the tree of life window, a pine tree with the pier cluster window, and wisteria with our wisteria window design. As a group, the students brainstorm how to make geometric patterns from organic shapes. For example, we show an image of a flower, tree, or bird, and as a group the students think about different geometric shapes that could be used to create the image and share those images on the classroom's whiteboard. A leaf might be composed of many triangles. A rose petal made of two half-circles. A tree trunk built of multiple rectangles. By doing this, the docent can gauge how much the students have understood about the organic nature of Wright's light screens, consider how much help students will need during the upcoming activity, and model for students a path to make their own design.

Following the PowerPoint and brainstorming part of the *Art Glass at the Martin House* program, students are given an opportunity to create their own light screens using a variety of materials including graph paper, Grafix clear cling vinyl film, permanent markers, rulers, pencils, and other drawing or measuring tools such as compasses, triangles, or protractors. Students

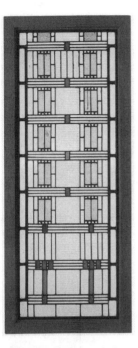

**Figure 11.2.  Wisteria Window.**
Collection Frank Lloyd Wright's Martin House, Buffalo, New York.

**Figure 11.3.  The American wisteria, *Wisteria frutescens*.**

are asked to think of an organic shape they can transform into a geometric window design. Some great examples from past groups have been fish, sunflowers, clouds, the sun, raindrops, waves, trees, and butterflies. Using graph paper, students start to use their drawing and measuring tools to make geometric shapes to represent their organic shape. Once the shape is one that they like, they lay the Grafix on top of the graph paper and trace the design with a permanent marker. Very carefully, they use different permanent markers to bring color to their design. Once complete, the Grafix paper can be adhered to a window simulating the light screen design. The permanent markers give their design a transparent look, almost like glass.

When researching the *Art Glass at the Martin House* program for the students, we investigated several questions. What inspired Frank Lloyd Wright to create light screens? In what ways are the Darwin D. Martin House windows innovative? How did Frank Lloyd Wright turn his idea of light screens into concrete form? To answer these questions, we investigated the design and construction of the Wright windows in a historical context and in contrast to typical windows of the time. Although art glass windows were popular in the early twentieth century, the Martin House showcases matchless designs.[6] We looked at how the organic architecture of the Martin House's windows was inspired by nature and harmony. Additionally, we considered how Wright's innovative idea to create windows as "light screens" required problem solving (choosing materials and planning for stability) and written and graphic skills (to communicate with artisans) for his idea to take form. Research focused on the areas of design, materials, and fabrication. To learn about the process for actually creating the light screens, we enlisted the help of local artisan Lawrence Tschopp, who provided valuable information about glass, caming, structural principles, and fabrication based on his extensive experience in restoring stained glass windows. It was from his studio that we were able to collect the hands-on materials used in the *Art Glass at the Martin House* program.

Once the background information was collected and teaching objects were gathered, we started thinking about implementation for various age groups, especially for outreach programming. The scalability of the program was important for us. While we want the majority of our participants to be able to visit the site and learn from the actual light screens, outreach opportunities are a significant component of our programming and we wanted this program to be available to a variety of audiences. We also wanted to make sure that participants could understand the history and design aspects of the windows of the Darwin D. Martin House without actually seeing them in person, although experiencing the original art glass is always preferred.

The *Art Glass at the Martin House* student program has gone through many renditions. The original objective of the activity has never changed: we always wanted students to understand that Wright used nature as his inspiration and designed window patterns that were geometric but based on organisms in nature. In the first iteration of this program, we had students sketch their individual ideas on paper and then transfer it over to the next medium like adhesive colored sheets and Mylar paper. This proved difficult as the colored sheets were expensive and hard to find, and the Mylar usually came in large sheets and needed to be cut. We then moved on to using tissue paper on construction paper, and while this made it easy to create the shapes, the final product was opaque and not transparent, and therefore did not resemble an art glass window. As with most program development, trial and error led to an improved product, and experimentation shaped our understanding of the available materials.

For our current program, we have the students design their windows on graph paper first as it helps to keep their shapes geometrically aligned. We have also settled on using Grafix cling vinyl film that comes in 9 × 12-inch sheet sizes along with permanent markers like those produced by Sharpie. Once they have designed their window on graph paper, they lay the cling vinyl film over it and "transfer" the design using the markers. Once the marker ink dries (only a few seconds) and the cling is held up to the light, it looks like a window. The students then take their self-created designs home, and the cling nicely "sticks" to one of their own windows creating the art glass, light screen effect.

As with any new program design, we were not sure how it would be received. Many teachers bring their students to the Darwin D. Martin House Complex to learn about local history as a strand of their social studies curriculum. How would an art activity coupled with a history lesson work for these teachers? What we found is that many classroom teachers were open-minded about the art activity, especially those who taught younger grades. There is so much history at the Martin House, and by focusing on one area like the history of the windows, the students have a unique and in-depth experience they can delve into. The teachers also appreciated the hands-on component of the program because it was something tactile the students could do at a historical site, which also appealed to English Language Learner teachers. The *Art Glass at the Martin House* program utilized a step-by-step knowledge-building approach that introduced new vocabulary and verbal directions with facilitated dialogue for students to participate in. An unintentional result was that participation in the *Art Glass at the Martin House* program introduced newly arrived citizens to an important cultural organization in Buffalo.

We found that most students enjoy this program very much, especially the classroom activity of handling art glass making pieces, working with tools, and designing their own window as an expression of their individual creativity. We continue to be impressed by the variety of organic shapes the students replicate according to Wright's geometric principles. The final products are always as unique as the student who created them. Our only challenge for the *Art Glass at the Martin House* program has been time. We usually allow one hour for the tour, and up to another hour for the art glass window–making activity. Given the constraints of a field trip, many schools do not have more than two hours to dedicate to this, although the students would continue working if they could.

There have been variations to the *Art Glass at the Martin House* program. For groups that have extended time at the site like the Martin House Summer Camp or a school group working over multiple days, they create large plastic windows that are then painted. Some classroom groups have translated their designs onto actual pieces of glass or plexiglass. A fifth grade class used their art glass design to complete a class project—one that reflected all of their unique and individual differences. The result included a geometric-designed hand, representing all of the students, holding up different designs in nature.

The major result of the *Art Glass at the Martin House* program has been an increase in visitation. Because the program can be easily adapted, we have seen an even larger variety of grade levels and subject area field trips. It has become a staple of our teacher professional development workshops, and we have offered it as a public program for adults who want to learn about and create their own versions of the Wright art glass windows. To date, it has become our most popular requested program outside of our traditional one-hour guided tour. We feel the *Art Glass at the Martin House* program has been a great way to expand our programming to connect history with art, as well as have our audience explore Frank Lloyd Wright's organic architecture design.

## NOTES

1. Donald Hoffmann, *Frank Lloyd Wright: Architecture and Nature* (New York: Dover, 1986).

2. Jack Quinan, ed. *Frank Lloyd Wright Windows of the Darwin D. Martin House* (Buffalo: Burchfield-Penney Art Center, 1999).

3. Alastair Duncan, *Tiffany Windows* (New York: Simon, 1980).

4. James L. Sturm, *Stained Glass from Medieval Times to the Present: Treasures to Be Seen in New York* (New York: Dutton, 1982).

5. Frederick S. Lamb, "The Making of a Modern Stained Glass Window: Its History and Process, and a Word about Mosaics," *The Craftsman* X, no. 1 (1906).

6. Eric Jackson-Forsberg, ed. *Frank Lloyd Wright: Art Glass of the Martin House Complex* (Petaluma: Pomegranate, 2009).

*Chapter Twelve*

# Cooking Up History
## *Learning from Gingerbread*
### Jean Neff

The Buffalo Niagara Heritage Village (BNHV), established as the Amherst Museum in 1972, is a thirty-five-acre open-air museum in the Town of Amherst, a suburb of Buffalo located in Erie County, New York. With a focus on the history of the town and the greater Buffalo Niagara Region, the museum uses eleven historic buildings, costumed interpreters, and museum exhibits to educate visitors about life in the nineteenth century. These buildings include period houses, a blacksmith shop, a barber shop, a church, and two different one-room schoolhouses. BNHV is home to a collection that numbers over 20,000 items, reflecting the domestic, agricultural, and industrial past of western New York with a specific emphasis on the Town of Amherst. This collection includes paintings, prints, furniture, ceramics, woodworking, metalworking, textiles, and textile-working tools.

Living history museums are known for experiential learning. Costumed interpreters, period rooms, and re-created homes are a staple of the experiences they offer. How, then, can other institutions learn from their programs? What can be borrowed to engage visitors in a broader understanding of historical content? The time period interpreted at the BNHV allows for programs that look at traditions across time and place. Topics that cross temporal and cultural boundaries resonate with today's visitors, and they are often exposed to history when they are not expecting it. Food, for example, is universal. Everyone consumes food for sustenance, but foodways are embodied with tradition and are rich in historical context and content.

Participants may not initially realize the amount of information one can learn from "simply" baking gingerbread. The process of baking can be used to teach cross-disciplinary content in world history, mathematics, English language arts, anthropology, geography, and local history. The topic of making something to eat is also approachable and of interest to a broad audience

**Figure 12.1.    The Buffalo Niagara Heritage Village's reconstructed Pioneer Kitchen.**
Courtesy of the Buffalo Niagara Heritage Village.

who may not otherwise identify as someone interested in a history lesson. Consequently, many historic house museums and historic sites have education programs that involve food. At the BNHV, a program that utilizes the site's reconstructed open-hearth kitchen is *Dutch Oven Gingerbread*, a popular, tasty, educational program that uses all five senses.

While many recipes have been lost to a primarily oral tradition, we do have the benefit of existing recipe books from the last two hundred years. Today, we have increased access to these ephemeral resources through online digitized sources. At the BNHV, the program utilized the book *Fanny Pierson Crane: Her Receipts, 1796*. This collection of eighteenth-century recipes was republished by the Montclair Historical Society in 1974 and includes a guide to open-hearth and beehive oven cooking. Drawn from the recipes of Fanny Pierson Crane, the matriarch of a prominent New Jersey family, this particular volume includes the eighteenth-century recipes with suggestions for modern-day adaptation and the addition of the suggested measurements for each ingredient, which we have included in the recipe below. While the BNHV chose to use this secondary source, there are a multitude of primary documents available as digital surrogates online. Searching for a publication that was used in your particular region will also add to the authenticity, relatability, and local history connections that can be made through the program. If archival material exists for a family known to have lived in your area, biographical information would also add to the program's narrative.

Fanny Pierson Crane's Dutch Oven Gingerbread recipe:

| | |
|---|---|
| 1 egg well beaten | ¼ teaspoon salt |
| ½ cup sugar | 1 teaspoon ginger |
| ½ cup dark molasses | 1 teaspoon cinnamon |
| ¼ cup butter | 1 teaspoon soda |
| ½ cup hot water | 1 tablespoon grated orange rind |
| 2 cups cake flour, sifted | |

Combine and beat well the egg, sugar, and molasses. Mix butter into hot water and stir until melted. Add butter mixture to sugar, egg, and molasses. Sift the dry ingredients together; add to other mixture in three parts, beating after each addition only until well blended. Pour into lightly greased mold. Bake in a covered Dutch oven for 40 to 50 minutes.

*Dutch Oven Gingerbread* utilizes inquiry-based learning techniques to engage the audience to have them discover connections between the recipe and history. At BNHV, it begins in the reconstructed kitchen, where participants are walked through the process of making gingerbread from start to finish. As the participants add each ingredient of the recipe, they are asked leading questions. Where did the ingredient come from? How would that ingredient have been acquired 150 to 200 years ago? Take for example the egg. Most families in western New York would have raised their own chickens, making eggs easily accessible. Another ingredient is butter, which is made from cream separated from the milk of a cow. Many families in this region would have had these domesticated animals. Flour was a staple for this recipe along with making daily bread. Early in the nineteenth century, farmers grew wheat and local gristmills were common, making it both accessible and inexpensive for early settlers.

If families did not have their own chickens, milk-producing animals, or wheat, the facilitator would ask how early settlers might get their groceries. This would open a discussion about the barter system. Early settlers would barter or trade for items like eggs and milk with neighbors who owned farms and had a surplus of these supplies.

The participants would be asked how else they might get these items if their neighbors did not have them. At this time, they would learn about the general store or mercantile and how other ingredients like baking soda would be available there. In early recipes, the leavening agent varied; in this example one teaspoon of baking soda is needed. Baking soda, or sodium bicarbonate, is a chemical compound that became available after two New Yorkers refined its development in 1846. Participants would also be asked what a family might do if they did not have the money or surplus items to trade until they received the raw materials to make goods to barter. This would, in turn, lead to a discussion about the credit system of a general store keeping a ledger of a family's transactions that would be "paid" later with either money or more likely other bartered goods.

The next question for the group would be how does the general store get its goods? With the opening of the Erie Canal, transportation improved allowing for goods to travel faster and cheaper from the east. The canal connected the Hudson River in Albany to Lake Erie in Buffalo. While there are some deposits of salt in the local western New York area, once the canal was completed in 1825, salt was brought by boat from an area around Syracuse, New York, nicknamed "Salt City." It became the top salt producer in the country during much of the nineteenth century due to its natural salt springs. Since some ingredients like sugar, molasses, and oranges could only be produced or grown in warmer climates than New York, they would have to be shipped to an eastern port like New York City and travel first north along the Hudson River until it reached the Erie Canal. Ginger and cinnamon are spices that came from Asia, halfway around the world. The distance these two ingredients would have to travel made them the most expensive in this particular recipe. If any of the above ingredients were unavailable or too extravagant, settlers would find suitable substitutions like maple sugar for white or brown sugar.

In addition to discussing the source of the ingredients, the lives of past Amherst residents were also part of the narrative. Because students from local schools are the most common audience for the *Dutch Oven Gingerbread*, there is an emphasis on the role children played in preparing food. Historically, the children in the family would have helped with many types of chores on the family farm. They would have taken care of the cows or animals. Older children would milk them, and even very young children would help to churn the butter. Another one of the many chores would have been for children to get water from the well. For this recipe, warm water was needed, and if the reconstructed open-hearth was a working one, it would be heated in a pot hung from a crane over the fire. After all the ingredients are discussed and mixed together, for this program rather than pouring the batter into a traditional Dutch oven, it is placed in a standard 9 × 13-inch cake pan and taken away to bake in a modern oven at 350° for about twenty-five to thirty minutes until done.

The reconstructed open-hearth kitchen of the BNHV is filled with reproductions of objects that would have been found in kitchens of the past.

The use of reproductions in this setting allows for easy and safe hands-on instruction. While a museum may have historical materials in the collection, they may be unavailable for programming use due to fragility, rarity, and accession status. Reproductions are useful tools to allow participants to fully explore an object that may be strange and unknown to them. During this program, while the gingerbread bakes, participants take turns examining the kitchen's objects. Leading questions are used to stimulate discussion among the group. What is it made of? Who would have made it? What do you think it was used for? How was it used? Object reading is a common pedagogical technique used in museums, and it is very beneficial in this program. For example, participants are shown an old, traditional Dutch oven made of cast iron that has a flat heavy lid with a lip around it and comes with legs. They are asked why the pot is designed this way. This is so it bakes food like an oven, with heat radiating from all sides. The hot coals would be put on top, and the lip of the lid would prevent them from slipping off. The legs allowed for coals to be placed up underneath. Today, Dutch ovens may or may not have legs depending on if they are used on stove burners, in ovens, or over wood when camping.

Kitchen objects with names no longer used present excellent examples to the participants of change over time. Some examples of this "extinct technology" shown to the participants are trammel, posnet, porringer, kneading box, butter churn, and reflector oven. If reproductions are unavailable, a few trips to local flea markets and antique stores can add to an educator's toolbox. Other objects in the kitchen that are still used today that perform the same function but appear very different are pointed out by the facilitator such as a toaster, pots, horn cup, and ladle. One example children are most familiar with that is still used today is a pizza peel.

Historical objects found outside of the kitchen can also be examined to reinforce the program. Rope bed, bed key, washboard, cradle, wooden shoes, boot jack, lanterns, candle box, candle mold, tin sconce, darning egg, and salt box are just some examples. Showing and explaining these everyday objects allows for the gingerbread to bake while adding to the historical content of the program. The discussion that ensues from the participants is oftentimes enlightening as each person brings their own unique upbringing and cultural perspective. Using these objects to stimulate discussion also allows time for the participants to share their own narrative within this context.

The conclusion of the *Dutch Oven Gingerbread* program is always the most memorable. Each participant (barring any known allergies) has a piece of warm gingerbread cake topped with whipped cream, a highlight of the day!

This program has also been conducted with two additional recipes: "Cup Cakes" and "Apple Slump." "Cup Cakes" comes from the 1833 book *The*

*American Frugal Housewife,* by Lydia Child. An "Apple Slump" recipe can be found in Marguerite Sharp's 1986 compendium of old recipes, *The Cook's Book: Including Bubble & Squeak and Apple Slump: and Many More Good Old-Fashioned Recipes.*

One of the strengths of this program is the ability to scale according to age and program duration. Younger students may enjoy reviewing children's songs of the time period and singing a rendition of "Bringing in the Sheaves" or "There's a Hole in My Bucket." Intermediate students may become engaged in a discussion of children's chores and how that relates to their current domestic requirements. Adults may enjoy all of these opportunities to harken back to a simpler time. Coupling this program with a more standard tour of the historic houses expands the object-based learning component to include the built environment.

To conclude, the program *Dutch Oven Gingerbread* is fun for facilitator and participant alike. Other popular hands-on learning programs that children could experience in concert with food-based programming at BNHV are old-fashioned toys and games and lessons in the one-room schoolhouse. Open-air museums have the facilities to be a historic microcosm of society. The diversity of structures and program offerings allows visitors to get a well-rounded view of what life was like during the interpreted time period. At the Buffalo Niagara Heritage Village, the focus is nineteenth-century rural New York State; however, these types of institutions can be found in many small towns and their resources are open and available for interpretation. That said, *Dutch Oven Gingerbread* can be done at home or in school. While the historical setting strengthens the message, the activity and corresponding discussion can happen anywhere. The history comes to light where you least expect it.

*Chapter Thirteen*

# Bound in History

## Handcrafting Books on the Roycroft Campus

Alan Nowicki and Amizetta Haj

The Roycroft Campus is a National Historic Landmark and birthplace of the American Arts and Crafts Movement. Located in East Aurora, New York, about nineteen miles southwest of Buffalo, it is the best preserved and most complete complex of buildings remaining in the United States of the "guilds" that evolved as centers of craftsmanship and philosophy during the late nineteenth century. The campus, designated a National Historic Landmark district in 1986, contains nine of the original fourteen structures including the Inn, the Chapel, the Print Shop, the Furniture Shop, and the Copper Shop. Its founder, Elbert Hubbard, was inspired by an 1894 trip to William Morris's Kelmscott Press in England and adopted the idea that books should be hand-crafted works of art. Morris is considered the father of the Arts and Crafts Movement, which was a rebellion against the emerging Industrial Revolution of the nineteenth century. Products that had been previously handmade were now being constructed by machines. Morris believed these products were poorly made, lacked style, and took away from the creative spirit of the workers. Hubbard returned to western New York emboldened with this new philosophy, wanting to replicate Morris's Kelmscott. He bought a press and built his first print shop in 1897 calling it the Roycroft Press. Hubbard, along with a handful of workers, began producing a monthly periodical called *The Philistine*, along with hand-bound copies of famous classical works.

In 1899, Hubbard needed filler for his March issue of *The Philistine* and wrote a story entitled "A Message to Garcia." In modern terms, the story "went viral." It was eventually translated into thirty-seven different languages, made into two movies, and became the third best-selling book at the time, behind only the Bible and the dictionary. Elbert Hubbard and the Roycrofters became known throughout the world. Within ten years, his shop grew into an art community of more than five hundred employees. Although the artists expanded to create a variety of products, such as furniture, leather goods, and decorative copper pieces, the primary focus of the Roycroft was the printing and binding of books. The campus eventually closed in 1938, due mainly to the effects of the Great Depression, having been one of the most successful and longest lasting Arts and Crafts communities in the world.

In the mid-1970s, the Roycroft entered a renaissance with a resurgence of the Arts and Crafts philosophy of well-designed, handmade crafts, and the goal of restoring the buildings on the campus was established. In 2015, the Roycroft Print Shop was reacquired, and some of the original printing presses were returned to the grounds. A museum was established in the building to help tell the story of the Roycroft and display examples of the original publications and books. Since then, demonstrations and hands-on workshops have been developed in printing, illumination, and bookbinding for guests visiting the campus.

As a group of associated historical buildings, the primary audience of the Roycroft Campus has been adults. The notion to expand programming to the P–12 classroom was seen as an opportunity to share the rich history of the Arts and Crafts Movement with a previously underserved audience. How then can students be encouraged to learn content at a historic site? Infusing the historical narrative into a multifaceted experience has been a successful model for the Roycroft. Thus began an interactive and ever-growing bookbinding program, *Bound in History*. Students are learning many facets of history, the process of historical inquiry, and content knowledge, and they are producing a tangible product of their own—a faux leather-bound journal. As Paul Johnson writes, "When children plan and design a book of their own, integrate handwriting, lettering, illustration, layout, and binding as a vehicle for the communication of ideas, a superior kind of mental activity comes into play."[1]

One expert who helped in the development of *Bound in History* was Diane Bond, a certified art educator and Roycroft Renaissance Master Artisan in book arts. She was a major resource in offering the history and process for a variety of book structures from different cultures and time periods, including single-sheet bookbinding, concertinas, Japanese stab binding, and Suminagashi, a form of paper marbling. Most importantly, Ms. Bond showed us the three-hole pamphlet stitch, the same technique used by the Roycrofters in binding *The Philistine.* She developed variations on this process so that different grade levels could be successful. As we began working with more schools, curriculum needs and suggestions from educators expanded the program and gave us the ability to develop class-specific projects.

Overall, the program gives students an understanding of books, their history, and how they are created, including the western New York influence on book arts. Tools and techniques are defined and used throughout the workshop for recognition. Students demonstrate their ability to follow instructions by creating one or more books using a variety of book structures, and they demonstrate their creativity to explore variations. Students also experience exemplar works of artisan-made books from both Roycroft history and contemporary times.

For the past few years, the Roycroft Campus has been working with eighth graders from a local school on one such bookbinding project. For the *Bound in History* program, prior to visiting the campus, the students study the Industrial Revolution and the immigration movement of the late nineteenth and early twentieth centuries in their social studies class. This is the same period that Elbert Hubbard was growing the Roycroft, and benefiting from the European craftsmen arriving in America in search of employment. Louis Kinder was one such artisan. Born and trained in Leipzig, Germany, one of the leading bookbinding centers of the world, Kinder moved to America and eventually found his way to Hubbard in 1896. He spent the next sixteen years establishing the Roycroft Bindery, training the young employees to become production binders, and eventually organizing a fine-binding section. Kinder produced works considered masterpieces in the art of bookbinding.

Upon arrival to the campus, students are presented with a brief history of Hubbard and the Roycroft, with an emphasis on writing and bookmaking. Leading questions are used to encourage group participation and dialogue. What is a book? What is its purpose? What is it made from? What are its parts? Some examples of unusually shaped books or those made from unconventional materials are shown to help students think outside of the box of their traditional understanding of these commonplace objects. The most common product used in the creation of a book is paper, and a single sheet is passed out to each student. Students are asked, What are some of the qualities of paper: size, color, texture, thickness? Can a single sheet of paper be a book? The students are taught some basic terms and tools associated with bookbinding, such as edge, fold, structure, and bone folder. Through a series of step-by-step procedures, the students fold and cut the paper until it is formed into a six-page book. The paper is preprinted with text, telling a short history of the book or of the Roycroft. Through this rather simple exercise, some of the basic terms and concepts of bookmaking are introduced.

Next, the group is shown examples of some original Roycroft publications, in particular, an edition of *The Philistine* is viewed. *The Philistine* was a monthly periodical written, printed, and published by Hubbard and his workers. It was pocket-size at 4½ × 6 inches in order to easily carry while traveling, and was hand-sewn using a three-hole pamphlet stitch. Following the same techniques the Roycrofters used to bind their magazines, the class creates their own bound journals.

**Figure 13.1.   Author Alan Nowicki works with a student at one of the presses.**
Courtesy of the Roycroft Campus.

Students select seven to ten pieces of standard-size paper and individually fold them in half, creasing each using a bone folder. The sheets are then placed one inside another until all the paper is nestled together. This is known as a signature or gathering. Students observe that the edges of the paper are starting to protrude out, and if additional pages were added they would stick out too far. Students are asked what would happen if a book has more than ten pages? Another Roycroft book is passed around, and students are asked to look at the edge of the pages near the spine. The pages seem to be making a series of "U" shapes. These are multiple signatures, which are sewn together to make a larger book. If they view their textbooks back at school, they were made in a similar way. For the campus workshop project, the book will have only one signature. A thicker sheet of paper is given out and folded to make an end paper. This is usually found in a book to give some protection to the inner pages, and the class places their gathering inside.

Next, the group is shown a bookbinding cradle. This tool looks like a baby cradle made of heavy cardboard or wood with two boards slanted toward each other in a "V" shape. The gathering is placed in the cradle so that it is opened to the middle page, and the sheets are clipped together on one side so they do not move. A template containing three holes is placed inside the signature so the edges line up. An awl, a thin hole-punching tool, is then used to poke a hole through all the pages of the signature and end paper. This is repeated for all three marks on the template.

Students can now select from a variety of precut, faux leather covers. The holes in the signatures are lined up with those on their cover, and a threaded needle is passed out to everyone. The three-hole pamphlet stitch is explained in a step-by-step procedure, as the class follows along. It is completed when the individual ties their final knot, binding their pages, end paper, and cover together, just as the Roycrofters did with *The Philistine*. A final faux leather strap is woven through the cover to tie the book closed.

After the field trip to the campus, the social studies teacher has the students use their handmade journals as one of their unit assessments. As one teacher stated:

> The Roycroft provides the students with an enriching educational experience by immersing them in this National landmark, learning about its history, and giving them a hands-on project, following the same procedure that was used over a hundred years ago. These journals will in turn be used back at school with a continuing project.

Back in the classroom, students create fictional identities. They pretend to be nineteenth-century immigrants coming to America and must create a manifest of personal information to board a ship, such as name, age, gender, occupation, destination, health, and education. The students visit the Ellis Island website and view authentic ship manifests. For the next three weeks in their social studies class, a writing prompt is given to the students, which they respond to in their handmade journals. Examples of the prompts include

**Figure 13.2.** A student works on her bookbinding project during a workshop at the Roycroft Campus.
Courtesy of the Roycroft Campus.

the following: Why do you want to leave Europe and go to the United States? What doubts are you having? What preparations will you make for the trip? What was your experience on the crowded ship? What was your reaction when you saw the Statue of Liberty for the first time? What was your experience on Ellis Island like? Later prompts include imagining what it was like as a new resident of the United States. Issues like prejudice, racism, and difficulties understanding the language are brought up. In their technology class, the students create imaginary passports, boarding passes, and maps to place in their journal. Students dress up as a turn-of-the-century immigrant and pictures are taken. Once completed, everything goes on display at the school for viewing by the rest of the school and parents.

This is a multidisciplinary project that relies on the established partnership between the individual teacher(s), the student, and the Roycroft Campus. That said, this project also has the ability to scale according to the available resources. It could all be done at the historic site or could be limited to the confines of the school district. Another aspect of this program is that it encourages repeat visitation or multiple visits. It allows for more than one isolated field trip, and the project is strengthened if built over time.

This project can be modified numerous ways. Students could base their journal on the experiences of an actual person. They could research the country of their own family origin, interviewing relatives and seeing if any photographs or documents exist. They could explore a historical figure, such as the Roycroft bookbinder Louis Kinder, or contact a local refugee agency to see if they could interview a recent migrant to America. From this research, the students could then create fiction or nonfiction diaries about the immigrant's journey to America.

For elementary students, modifications were created to simplify this bookbinding process. To do so, local book artists researched and designed a variety of book structures for students to make, which correspond with the historical or cultural needs of a teacher's curriculum. Teachers have commented there is increased interest of students to write in a book that they have made themselves. While the narrative and research aspect of the program is stressed here, another modification for younger audiences is to have students draw their experience if writing is not advanced.

These projects have also expanded to include additional activities. Students can receive a tour around the Press Room and learn about typesetting, the California Job Case that holds the lead type, and the printing presses. They are led through the process of selecting a font from a type cabinet, using a composing stick, preparing the chase, and locking up the type. The locked chase is set into either a Pearl or Chandler & Price press, and a demonstration follows. Each student can have a chance to run the press using their own foot power and create a printed page from one of the original Roycroft presses. Set aside to dry for a few hours, these prints can be taken by the students as a keepsake or bound into their handmade book.

Another option is a class visit to the Illumination Studio. Illuminations harken back to the Middle Ages, when monks were creating handwritten books in which the text was enhanced with such decorations as large initial letters, borders, and miniature illustrations. These designs would then be colorfully painted and highlighted with silver or gold leaf. Many of the ideas of the Arts and Crafts Movement look back to the medieval period and the guild system. Books from both Morris's Kelmscott Press and the Roycroft were often filled with hand illuminations, which could inspire students with creative designs of their own. These hand-painted illuminations could be used as a project by itself or combined with their book project.

To further enrich these programs, we look to expand the use of primary sources from the campus's museum and give additional historical information on some of the original Roycroft artists. A pre-visit to the classroom or admission to the museum could include a viewing of the March 1899 edition of *The Philistine*, the issue that contained the very first printing of "A Message to Garcia." The book *Little Journeys to the Homes of English Authors* contains a hand-illumed title page, designed by Samuel Warner. This edition is #800 of #947 copies printed and illumed at the Roycroft in 1899. Other items could include photographs, handwritten letters, furniture, paintings, sculpture, and copper work.

The Roycroft, and the Arts and Crafts Movement as a whole, is an interesting counterpoint to the Industrial Revolution. Hubbard was also very vocal with his beliefs on social issues, women's rights, and a strong work ethic—all important topics both then and now. As one social studies teacher whose class visited the campus stated, "The Roycroft is such an asset to the western New York community. Students should be exposed to this local history, and how it connects back to the topics we are studying in school." With the continuing restoration of the Roycroft Campus buildings, fully operational nineteenth-century printing presses, and growing list of interactive workshops, our aim is to inspire students and guests with the ideals of the Arts and Crafts Movement. This National Historic Landmark has been revived as a center for art and learning, and education will be the catalyst for the Roycroft Campus to once again be an international cultural destination.

## NOTE

1. Paul Johnson, *Literacy through the Book Arts* (Portsmouth, NH: Heinemann, 1993), 13–14.

*Chapter Fourteen*

# History Around the Block
## *Neighborhood Archaeology*
### Elizabeth S. Peña and Kristen Gasser

Can students learn about people in the past by examining what materially remains in the present? The challenge of conducting an archaeological investigation provides rich pedagogical opportunities to cultivate curiosity, encourage close observation, hone critical-thinking abilities, and develop broad-based skills (in reading, writing, and math). Class field trips to archaeological excavations in exotic locales may be unlikely, but students can practice archaeological thinking in their own classrooms, around their own neighborhoods, and even on their own block.

Many communities may not have the luxury of their own history museum or other cultural institutions, but this should not exclude anyone from implementing site-based strategies to learn about the past. All communities have neighborhoods. While their appearance and geographical boundaries may differ, they can still be used to learn history and engage participants in the discovery and interpretation of a historical narrative.

A collaboration between educational program developers and museum curators at the Buffalo Museum of Science in the 1990s resulted in the creation of two projects designed to use archaeology as a way to engage middle school students and their teachers in hands-on, inquiry-based learning: (1) *Digging Archaeology* (part of a series entitled "Object Lessons"), an in-class simulated dig based on an actual archaeological site, and (2) *Neighborhood Archaeology*, which uses "above-ground archaeology" to encourage students to ask questions, gather information, and evaluate evidence about the history of their own local area by following archaeological principles.

Both of these projects empower students to "be" archaeologists, heightening their interest in history and culture while introducing, and having them practice, a wide variety of academic skills. *Digging Archaeology* is organized as a mystery to be solved by the students, as they follow hints revealed in maps, replica artifacts, photographs, and other materials. As the project proceeds, more information is revealed, as it would be on an archaeological dig. Students evaluate the evidence and weigh the clues. While the "right" answer (the type of site) is revealed at the end of the project, it is the process itself, in which students practice critical thinking, that is of most value. This program is one of four "Object Lessons" kits—"Inquiries into Natural and Cultural History." The unit is still in use in a number of school districts and museums and comes complete with a full set of materials and standards-based lesson plans, designed for use in middle school classrooms (www.firsthandlearning .org).

Committed to designing programs and pedagogical environments that promote learning from direct experience and original sources, the project developers wanted to offer another way for teachers to use archaeology for inquiry and exploration without the need to invest in the kit, *Digging Archaeology*, and without the need for extensive professional development. Drawing on the expertise of the museum's resident archaeologist, the collaborative team developed strategies that would allow teachers and students to conduct authentic, inquiry-based archaeological investigations in the immediate area around their school. The key to the development of this new project, which came to be *Neighborhood Archaeology*, was an understanding of the broad range of archaeological methods and an appreciation of the term "artifact." First, while the common image of archaeologists digging is certainly true, archaeologists acquire data using a combination of below-ground and above-ground methods; it would be entirely appropriate to develop an educational program using an accessible above-ground technique. Second, in studying artifacts, archaeologists do not always work with tiny sherds and fragmentary pieces. Artifacts can also be large, complex objects, based on the definition of an artifact as anything made, modified, or moved by human agency. *Neighborhood Archaeology* was then designed around an accessible above-ground method of doing archaeology, with an accessible artifact type—the house, or more broadly speaking, the built environment.

*Neighborhood Archaeology* can be adapted to suit a wide variety of circumstances ranging from desired learning objectives to educational levels to the physical setting of the school itself. Importantly, *Neighborhood Archaeology* brings students out of the classroom and around the block, making them aware of the active presence of history in their own lives, outside of their classrooms and textbooks.

In the 1990s, the Buffalo Museum of Science housed the Center for Science Learning, led by Peter B. Dow, which received funding from the National Science Foundation to support intensive teacher professional development in science. Through the Teacher Education at the Museum (TEAM) program, teachers were exposed to the resources of the museum and learned about the processes of scientific inquiry partly through field and laboratory activities led by museum staff. "Object Lessons" kits were also initially developed by the Center for Science Learning with grant funds from the Howard Hughes Medical Institute. This work continued, with additional funding from the National Science Foundation, when the Center for Science Learning left the Buffalo Museum of Science in 1998 to form Firsthand Learning, Inc.

The mission of Firsthand Learning, Inc. is to promote the process of scientific inquiry as a vehicle for learning. To this end, Firsthand Learning, Inc. designs and implements curriculum materials and professional development programs that emphasize direct, firsthand experiences with natural and cultural phenomena. While the focus of *Neighborhood Archaeology* is historical, its basis is in the field of historical archaeology, which relies on the scientific method (observation, data collection, hypothesis testing, etc.). Because of this, *Neighborhood Archaeology* is allied with the arts and humanities as well as with the sciences.

The key to developing both *Digging Archaeology* and *Neighborhood Archaeology* was the collaboration between Firsthand Learning, Inc. and the Buffalo Museum of Science. The *Neighborhood Archaeology* activities were produced initially as professional development experiences for Buffalo Public School teachers involved in the TEAM project. Kristen Gasser, then Project Coordinator at the museum's Center for Science Learning (and later Director of Publications at Firsthand Learning, Inc.), brought the educational framework to the project; Elizabeth S. Peña, then Curator of Anthropology at the Buffalo Museum of Science, brought the archaeological content. This combination ensured that the program was both useful and meaningful.

Archaeology is the study of how people lived in the past based on things and places they left behind. As one of the subfields of anthropology, archaeology is broadly concerned with the study of the human condition in the past. In this way, archaeology can investigate periods of time before the advent of the written record. Archaeologists specializing in more recent eras use the documentary record as an important information source, moving back and forth between the archives and archaeological evidence. In North America, the field of historical archaeology deals with the time period beginning with the European arrival in North America, continuing through the twenty-first century.

For archaeologists, artifacts represent the physical manifestation of culture; reading the cultural cues that are encoded in artifacts provides insight into culture. *Neighborhood Archaeology* uses an archaeological perspective to investigate above-ground artifacts, in this case, houses. The documentary record (historical maps, city directories, census records, etc.) provides additional information that, along with the physical evidence, helps piece together a picture of the past.

Archaeologists begin with questions: How did people live in the past? What did they eat, what did they wear, what were their families like? In what ways were they similar to us, living here today? How were they different? Encouraging students to ask questions like these can help them develop an awareness and appreciation of culture as a relevant construct, and history as a continuum in which they themselves have a role to play.

Using basic scientific principles and an "archaeological eye," observations become data, which serve to confirm or negate hypotheses. The leap from data to interpretation is a complicated matter and a constant concern for all archaeologists. It leads to the epistemological question, "How do we know what we know?" To provide structure to data collection, archaeologists create hypotheses, or statements, that can be examined with the available data. The goal of research is not necessarily to confirm a hypothesis, but to use a hypothesis to guide the research process and to generate ideas. Hypotheses are refined and regenerated as the collected data are analyzed in conjunction with archaeological interpretation. After the data are gathered, their analysis and interpretation depend upon the archaeologists' understanding of the relationship between the data and the "big picture," that is, larger historical trends. Of course, archaeologists are also influenced by prevailing theoretical perspectives, politics, and their own cultural biases. While the facts might remain constant, there may be as many interpretations as there are interpreters.

Since *Neighborhood Archaeology* relies on an "above-ground archaeology" approach of examining buildings, the project is most easily conducted in a walkable neighborhood with houses; in fact, the project was developed by the authors over a number of slow, observant walks around the Buffalo Museum of Science's East Side neighborhood. *Neighborhood Archaeology* introduces students to the principal steps of archaeological investigation: the creation of hypotheses, well-documented investigation and observation, the search for patterns, and the proposal of interpretations.

Learning objectives for *Neighborhood Archaeology* might include these: Use basic scientific principles and observations to confirm or negate hypotheses. Learn to "read" objects and generate scientific questions based on those observations. Study architectural principles. Learn about trends in local history. The following lesson outline, which is meant for teacher training purposes, is open for adaptation based on the needs of the teacher and the class.

### The Scenario

In order to learn more about how your school fits into its community, you have received a grant to conduct a study of the neighborhood around the school. Now you have to decide how to initiate the project.

**Figure 14.1.** The Humboldt Parkway neighborhood in Buffalo, New York, has a rich variety of house styles.
Courtesy of the Buffalo Museum of Science.

### The Project
What is your first step? You will need to decide on the project's goals. What is the point of the study? What are our hypotheses? Some examples: (1) the school was one of the first properties in the neighborhood and was the impetus for neighborhood growth; (2) the neighborhood architecture reflects the significance of the local brickmaking industry; or (3) the social and economic status is reflected in domestic architecture, including intra-neighborhood house locations and architectural detail.

### The Process
Each hypothesis can be broken down into practical, manageable units. For example, for hypothesis number three, the following questions might be posed: Are larger houses located on hilltops, with smaller houses at the bottom of the hill? Do larger houses display greater architectural detail, including door surrounds, decorative front porches, and stairs? Do larger houses have more elaborate gardens and greener yards?

### Data Collection
How will we conduct the study in order to address these questions? What information will we record? Using maps, notebooks, and/or data collection sheets, we might choose to record house size/location, materials, door surrounds,

**Figure 14.2. House styles can vary greatly in one city block, as seen here in the Humboldt Parkway neighborhood of Buffalo, New York.**
Courtesy of the Buffalo Museum of Science.

fenestration details, front porch description, lighting, plantings, edging and gardens, or driveway type. Usually, archaeologists have the responsibility of recording all potentially meaningful information for the use of future researchers. For example, our study would not require us to record the colors of front doors, but that information might be relevant to another researcher. We need to decide on the "sampling universe," or our study boundaries. Our options include both *nonprobabilistic* and *probabilistic* sampling strategies.

*Nonprobabilistic* sampling involves decisions based on pragmatic considerations, intuitive knowledge, and historical documentation. For example, if we are only interested in two-story houses, and we know that Oak Street only has ranch-style homes, it would be counterproductive to include Oak Street in our study. We might rely on tax maps and other existing information to move our survey to Pine Street, which we know is characterized by two-story structures.

In contrast, one of the goals of *probabilistic* sampling is to use a small sample to predict a larger one. There are three basic forms of probabilistic sampling: *random, systematic, and stratified.*

- *Random* sampling involves dividing the study area into smaller units, then investigating a predetermined number of units. The units chosen for study are selected from a table of random numbers or a similar method. For example, we might divide our study area into ten units, with four houses in each unit. Each unit would be numbered, one through ten, and we would put pieces of paper numbered one through ten in a hat. If we had agreed to sample four units, we would draw four numbers out of the hat to identify our sample. In our fieldwork, we would record information for only those houses within the boundaries of our four preselected units.

• *Systematic* sampling also includes a random element, as the first unit of study is chosen randomly. Additional units are selected at regular intervals. For example, after picking our first unit, we might agree to sample every fourth unit within our study universe. We would record information for the houses in every fourth unit, skipping all other houses.

• *Stratified* sampling allows for some refinements. The sampling universe can be divided into zones; within each zone, units of study are selected randomly. For example, if we are most interested in hypothesis number three, we might want to take this approach. The equal-sized zones we delineate might be based on topography; for example, one zone would be at the top of a hill, another at the bottom, with a third zone in between. This coverage might best test our hypothesis.

## Discussion

We also need to consider the parameters of the grant in our project scenario. What will available funds cover? How many field staff do we have? How much time? All of these factors will affect our selection of a study area. Let's suppose we've selected a principal hypothesis, a study area, and a sampling strategy. To facilitate data recording, we might want to create a standard form that all project members can use. In this way, the data gathered by different people at different times will be reasonably consistent. In developing the form, we must consider carefully the information that we would like to have, bearing in mind that characteristics that seem noteworthy to one person might be overlooked by another. The form will provide spaces for notes in specific categories, ensuring an overall consistency. In a further attempt to reduce subjectivity, rubrics will be created to guide the completion of the form. People will work in teams of at least two; teamwork provides an additional check to idiosyncrasy. Despite these efforts to obtain objective results, some degree of human subjectivity is inherent in the process. In future fieldwork, the form can be refined to reduce its flaws and increase standardization.

## Examination

Once the field survey is completed, we need to organize and examine our data. While most archaeologists would use a computer database that allows for manipulation and inquiry, we can tally results on a chalkboard or overhead projector. For each sample area, we can record the number of two-story houses, the number of houses with plantings in the number one range, and so on.

We would also want to mark the locations of the studied properties on a map. A simple way to do this would be to use transparencies of maps, coloring in all the houses with door detail number two in blue, all houses with door detail number three in red, and so on. The varying transparencies can be placed over one another, providing a clear visual impression of similarities and differences in the study area.

Archaeologists might use various statistical tests to determine if the differences between sample areas are significant (this might be useful if teachers want to use math, with a chi square test, for example). What questions do we want to ask of our data? To get closer to our hypothesis, we would want to compare the characteristics of the houses in three sampling areas (hilltop, base of hill, and in between). To accomplish this goal, we need a summary of each area, perhaps in a table, chart, or map overlay.

Suppose we find that the hilltop houses have longer property lines, more windows, more elaborate door details, but simpler plantings than the other two groups. What might account for this? Why would the people with "simpler" houses have more elaborate plantings? Is it a way for them to try to aggrandize their homes within their own means (rather than enlarging the structure of the houses)? Are they in some fashion trying to emulate the "better" homes on the hilltop? Or do they operate just within the limits of their own zone, ignoring the hilltop homes? Perhaps their garden displays are how they rank themselves within their own small area.

How could we gather more information to understand this more clearly? Perhaps we could revisit that sampling area with new, more detailed questions about flowers, specific plants, garden sculptures, and so on. The important concept is that the choices people make in the creation of their plantings reveal something significant about their worldview and how they see themselves. The gardens, as cultural artifacts, are "recursive"—they are both the product and the medium of human behavior.

This is an example of an investigation into the elite and non-elite of society, the relationship between these groups, and how the non-elite operate. Do they emulate the elite, or are there competing hegemonies between the elite and non-elite? For this exercise, one part of the group may develop a detailed data sheet for examining plantings in the hilltop area, another in the intermediate area, and another for the zone at the base of the hill. For example, we may want to record the types and quantities of flowers. Back in the lab, we might want to look up the prices of the annuals in a catalog to see the relative expenditure of each household on annuals. What might this mean? Did the hilltop homeowners spend more on annuals than other groups? If so, what might this mean? If not, what are some possible interpretations? When we compare the information from each group, we can come up with a more in-depth interpretation than was possible in our initial survey. Our scope may have narrowed (from looking at house facades and front properties to focusing on the plantings or gardens), but the rich information we have gathered will give our research more interpretive power.

If we were to plan future seasons of fieldwork, we could focus on different aspects. For example, we might decide to schedule our next season for a detailed comparison of front porches and how they are used within each separate study area. Is there porch furniture? A decorative flag? Flowerpots?

To conclude, this complex teacher's guide is meant to be adapted for classroom use. For instance, a simple walk around the neighborhood boundaries would be a good start, asking students to be keen observers and inviting them to draw and write notes in their journals to document their observations. In the classroom, a discussion of these notes might lead to a map made by the class as a whole, or by student teams. Whether students might be led toward generating hypotheses (What do we want to learn? What do we think or assume?) and creating questions to test those hypotheses on future excursions is up to the teacher, the level of the students, and many other factors.

Teachers can modify *Neighborhood Archaeology*, using its ideas and principles to meet the needs of their own lesson plans with respect to learning outcomes, time, effort, and budget. *Neighborhood Archaeology* can help enliven history by making students realize that history is not a distant concept; rather, it is around the block and in the neighborhood, and the students themselves are active agents.

*Chapter Fifteen*

# A Peek Beyond the Veil

## Spiritualist Shorts at Lily Dale

Amanda Shepp

The Marion H. Skidmore Library is located inside the Lily Dale Assembly in Lily Dale, New York. Since its early beginnings in 1879, Lily Dale has become the largest and longest continually operating Spiritualist camp in the United States, hosting a rich history of Spiritualist religion and culture while providing a unique glimpse into a religion that once swept the nation. In 1886, one of Lily Dale's founding members, Marion Skidmore, started a tent library outside of her home from a combination of her own personal collection of books and donations from authors and lecturers who visited Lily Dale in its formative years. By 1888, the book collection had outgrown the tent and was given a permanent indoor space on the second floor of a building called Library Hall where it resided for nearly forty years as it continued to expand. Eventually, the collection grew enough to necessitate the construction of a dedicated library building, which was completed in 1923 and still houses the collections of the Marion H. Skidmore Library today. The library houses rare books, periodicals, and archival ephemera, as well as a rich collection of materials created by modern Lily Dale residents and visiting authors. It is widely regarded as the largest library of materials about and relating to Spiritualism in the world.

In the fight to stay relevant, libraries are always expanding their offerings and breaking the mold as the traditional storehouse for old books. As a special library, the niche subject matter adds another barrier to some visitors' desire to engage with the facility and its collection, as well as potentially impeding the perception that they are allowed to do so. While libraries are known to house historical resources, their place as a platform for programming may be less obvious to the uninitiated. I wanted to offer programming at the library beyond providing access to the collection and functioning as a tourist information center. How could we draw attention to our rare and unique materials

**Figure 15.1. Entrance to Lily Dale Spiritualist community, New York.**
Image by Christopher Shepp.

with the summer season visitors in a way that would let them feel connected to these books?

As the newly minted librarian, I looked to offer programming that welcomed a new audience into the library every summer while also highlighting the resources we had to offer. The library holds twenty-eight thematic collections grouped into topics that relate to Spiritualism. I wanted to make sure that these themes and their interrelatedness were covered to draw attention to the historical magnitude of Spiritualism in its heyday, as this would allow for a very diverse array of materials and subjects to be highlighted. It felt only natural to do a short-format lecture series during the Lily Dale Assembly summer season. The tradition of lectures in Lily Dale is longstanding, having been one of the foundational elements in the creation of many Spiritualist camps of the late 1800s. This presented me with a challenge: How could this nineteenth-century format be appealing to twenty-first-century visitors?

Lifelong learning is a tenet of the Spiritualist religion, and while many workshops and learning activities are centered around developing one's own skills or connecting with the past, there are few that are offered regularly on Spiritualist history rather than Spiritualist practice, belief, philosophy, or development. The ample selection of historical materials at the Marion

H. Skidmore Library, many collected from the first years of the Lily Dale camp by Skidmore herself, provided a near infinite selection of topics and historical figures to choose from to provide a wide array of unique weekly topics throughout the summer camp seasons. Reducing the lecture format to "shorts" added freshness to the programming and allowed for guests to be introduced to the content in smaller, more manageable portions.

Originally, *Spiritualist Shorts* were designed for the average visitor to the Lily Dale Assembly—namely, adults with a strong desire to learn. After the first year of *Spiritualist Shorts*, the audience grew to include a much wider age range that often included older teens, young adults in their twenties, and senior citizens—including a lovely woman celebrating her ninety-first birthday who attended the *Spiritualist Short* about women's suffrage and its connection to Spiritualism. The diversity of the audience was proof that the format was what current lifelong learners were looking for. Since the program's inception, *Spiritualist Shorts* have been given to various community clubs, college students, historical societies, academic groups, and even elementary school students—the wonderful thing about "show and tell" is that it is completely scalable. The short-format nature of *Spiritualist Shorts* allowed for them to be included in a variety of events and programs outside of the Marion H. Skidmore Library, such as Rotary Club luncheons, League of Women Voters dinners, and presentations for classes of college students across western New York. The shorts were also reworked into content for living history tours around Chautauqua County.

Initially, the objective of *Spiritualist Shorts* was to have the average Lily Dale summer visitor gain a better understanding of the rich and complex history of Spiritualism and its related beliefs and practices. The goal was to help visitors understand the context of Spiritualism's growth within the nationwide development and industrial expansion of the United States, in a way that would be relevant, comprehensible, and interesting. Due to its invention in the mid-nineteenth century, the key tenets of this relatively new religion are inexorably intertwined with core beliefs of innovation, curiosity, and exploration that were proliferated in the culture of Victorian-era industrialization. To better understand the popularity and rapid growth of Spiritualist beliefs is to better understand the zeitgeist of America as a country barely a century in age—the desire for newness and cultural exploration, the eschewing of tradition in favor of amalgamated beliefs, and the urge to carve out a new and distinctly non-Colonial identity for itself. This philosophy was especially true in New York State, where Spiritualism originated, due to the boom of new religious faiths and philosophies that prevailed in the Burned-Over District of central and western New York State and were spread via railways and the Erie Canal through industrial routes to other major metropolitan areas.

The intent of *Spiritualist Shorts* expanding visitors' understanding of Spiritualism seemed apparent and successful as indicated by the amount of great questions, comments, and participation from attendees. What was unexpected was the added bonus of the *Shorts* being personally relevant to many attendees and library patrons, which often sparked the desire to attend the talk in the first place. Many summer visitors to Lily Dale travel from across New York State, and the history of the Spiritualist movement being so entrenched in the state's historical narrative means that an element of the *Short* frequently resonates with the local audience and strengthens their understanding of the material. In the case of *Spiritualist Shorts*, the widespread history of Spiritualism and related topics covered, as well as the materials chosen to have the audience interact with, provided ample opportunities to connect with patrons from across the country and allow them to see their own local history in a new way that was personally relevant and interesting to them.

As with most newly developed programs, the process was one of evolution. In my first year at the Marion H. Skidmore Library, I put together a traditional library tour that showcased many of the more interesting and unique artifacts in the collections, which proved to be very popular. Building on these tours, in preparation for the next season, I chose to research some of these showcased items further, highlighting their creators and their related philosophies in more depth in order to offer a weekly series. I also extended invitations to colleagues to fill weekly spots with their own short-format, non-workshop, educational talks related to Spiritualist topics. I set out with the intent to create short-format talks that adhered to a thirty-minute time frame, as this would allow me to take advantage of a time window where there was no competing programming happening at the Lily Dale Assembly. I wanted to create a more contemporary lecture format in order to give deeper attention to a niche topic without it being a serious academic endeavor: the oratory equivalent of a Wikipedia article, each complete with a snappy title that would pique interest and stand out in the large brochure of Lily Dale Assembly's summer events and workshops. This way, *Shorts* would be fun for me to research and deliver in an informal tone while being interesting and fast-paced enough to keep the audience engaged and leave them wanting to learn more about the topic on their own. Ideally, it could be a great way to get the average person interested in our highly specialized collections, and would spread the word about the huge variety of resources available at the Marion H. Skidmore Library.

In deciding topics for the *Spiritualist Shorts*, I first made sure the focus was something personally interesting. If I found the topic, person, or concept interesting enough to research, surely somebody would find it interesting enough to listen to for thirty minutes. It made the talk fun to research and easy to deliver because I could let my passion for the topic steer the pace and attitude of the lecture material. I liked to choose subjects that were provocative and interesting, frequently misunderstood (especially within their own field or their own time, and even more so by modern scholars), or related to a piece of popular culture or modern social element. These parameters made the lectures relatable to attendees, and served to keep them engaging—not to trot out a tired cliché, but they made history come alive in a way that was fresh and new rather than forced.

After I decided upon the theme of the *Spiritualist Short*, I considered what sources would best illustrate this person or subject. In the process of scanning the collections for possible materials to "show and tell," I would choose books that could stand up to handling, and would often choose books that were eye-catching in some way: gilt-embossed or illustrated covers, filled with many plates and illustrations, signed by a relevant figure, or unique in some other way. I wanted to literally put history in people's hands and give them a chance to forge a personal connection with these objects in the same way that I had in my time working with them as a librarian—the curiosity that sparks when cataloging a particularly beautiful book and wanting to know its story, inspiring the desire to know more about the objects that one comes in contact with on a regular basis. It gives the audience members a sense of responsibility when they are handed a rare book, to know that a fragile and often irreplaceable piece of their own history is in their hands and that this history needs to be taken care of and appreciated lest it be forgotten.

This drive to experiment with library-fueled historical lectures ultimately led to me delivering six of the first ten *Spiritualist Shorts* based on library materials, and the remaining four were delivered by guest speakers. The guest speakers were fairly unique in that their lectures also highlighted materials in our collections by supplementing their lecture content or presenting a more detailed illustration of a particular concept. For example, a lecture on Victorian flower readings was enhanced by showcasing Victorian-era instructional pamphlets on flower reading and other "social séance" methods. This particular lecture ended with an interactive demonstration of how these readings were performed, with participants drawing flowers from a bouquet and receiving their own Victorian-style flower readings. For my portions that were based on the library's collections, I selected the materials that had initially inspired the *Shorts* along with any other supplementary collection materials that could help give context to the artifact. During the talk, these materials were passed along to the group members, who circulated the materials among themselves until the end of the *Short*. The initial run of the *Spiritualist Shorts* series was well-received, with many visitors attending what turned out to be one of very few free programs to attend in Lily Dale, and many completing the visitor surveys with positive comments and creative suggestions for pro-spective topics for the future.

The *Spiritualist Shorts* for the following summer were all focused on the library collections and given by me, with some guest speakers returning for an extended program of their own rather than as a part of the *Spiritualist Shorts* series. Due to the need to fill all of the slots on my own, I chose to revise and reuse some of the talks from the previous year, as this would also give returning summer guests who did not get the chance to experience the initial run of *Spiritualist Shorts* in their premiere year the opportunity to do so. This format proved to be successful, and I continued to repeat about half of the *Shorts* used in the prior year for the upcoming summer season. The *Shorts* that were based on library collections varied widely in subject, and allowed the opportunity to mine the twenty-four subject-based collections for unique and interesting sources as well as eye-catching rare books or books with rich illustrations that would help illuminate the given topic from a his-torical perspective.

To better illustrate how each of the talks was conceived and created, I will discuss the process used to craft my favorite of the *Spiritualist Shorts*, "Books Beyond the Veil: Channeled Works at the Marion H. Skidmore Library." This particular presentation was the first *Spiritualist Short* and is based in part on an exhibition of channeled books that was loaned to a nearby university in an effort to cross-promote our collections. To clarify, channeled books are works allegedly created through a medium by a person who is considered to be no longer among the living. In WorldCat, these books are often misattributed to the deceased author, or have the medium listed as the primary author, when technically these two entities are co-authors of a given work. The amount of incongruencies in the cataloging information inspired a deeper look at their bibliographic information, which was often fraught with problems and instilled a desire to correct this perception about channeled works in a widespread format. More than this, I wanted to demonstrate the huge variety of methodologies by which these works are thought to have been created; channeled books can be transcribed with stenographers, written via spiri-tual communication devices like spirit trumpets or Ouija boards, and could feature famous historical figures or celebrities of years gone by. By modern standards, many channeled books are seen as gimmicky or laughable, but as the *Short* discusses, at the time of their release, many of these works were innovative and provocative, even scientific, and provided a form of evidence to the average person that there is something waiting for us in the afterlife.

The books discussed in this *Short* were chosen because they stood out during the cataloging process. Many of the titles are rare books or pieces of original cataloging and host truly interesting content. Some have relevance in the history of Spiritualism, and others showcase the unique nature of Spiritualist materials that have been credited to authors who are long passed on. While I was cataloging a copy of *Oahspe*, a Bible-style text that was written by a Baltimore dentist in 1880, the unique features of the book (text divided in half horizontally to sandwich two books into one, incredibly detailed plates and pull-out maps of spiritual realms, and very limited cataloging information on WorldCat) inspired me to do some deeper research on this object. After learning more about the book itself, its creator, and its very limited initial publication, I learned that many of these channeled books come with their own unique backstories—and I wanted these stories to be heard and appreciated by more people than other librarians and deeply involved researchers.

In order to demonstrate the variety of channeled and spirit writings held in the Marion H. Skidmore Library's collections and to give a rounded representation to the myriad ways in which the deceased supposedly communicate and collaborate with still-living authors, the books selected are exemplary of each major type of spiritual communication. This would also allow for a retrospective lecture on channeled works, as the methods of alleged spiritual communication tended to get more complex and mechanical as the religion of Spiritualism gained followers and popularity during its heyday, which would give the lecture itself some natural structure and pacing. With this in mind, works selected to illuminate this concept in the *Short* included works thought to be written through slate writing (*Between the Slates*, a book written describing séance activity in Lily Dale during the 1920s), spirit trumpets (*A Book for Skeptics*, describing activity in a family-run seance attraction in the early 1850s when Spiritualism was new), and trance (*Psychopathy, or Spirit Healing*, a work written by internationally famous medium Cora Richmond during the Golden Age of Spiritualism, approximately 1860–1910). Also included in the *Short* are channeled works that were once nationally celebrated or were attributed to well-known figures: *The Sorry Tale* (a channeled work that inspired numerous franchise material such as radio dramas, children's books, and even dolls—and was ultimately found to be a hoax), *Voices from the Spirit World* (a piece from Isaac Post, the head of the family responsible for spreading the news and fame of the Fox Sisters as they originated Spiritualism), and *Pen Pictures* (a book allegedly written by the spirits of Robert Burns and library founder Marion Skidmore, gossiping about life at the Lily Dale Assembly during the turn of the twentieth century). While somewhat varied in publication date and content, these works proved to be an entrancing journey through the history of perceived communication with the deceased, and were often subsequently requested for a closer look from the attendees.

I still give the *Spiritualist Shorts* when given the chance to do so. I use them to teach about niche historical fads like phrenology and to discuss social movements like Freethought to students and members of State University of New York College at Fredonia's History Club, and also as educational entertainment for groups such as Rotary Clubs or Brown Bag lectures. Because of the "show and tell" nature of these talks, they can be given using a variety of resources to illustrate points or illuminate concepts. For example, in a biographical lecture about Sir Arthur Conan Doyle, I use a clip of an interview with him on YouTube in which he discusses his Spiritualist beliefs. Digital collections are also very useful for off-site hacks of these short-format talks, and I have found them to be a great enhancement to the type of special collections outreach achieved through these *Shorts*. When I wanted to discuss a particular book that was not in the collection, especially a notably illustrated book or a book that embodied a critical work in a talk about an author, I would find a digital facsimile of that book and would either pass around a tablet with that digitized book ready for browsing or show specific pages from the book on a projector screen. During the *Shorts* that were given off-site for luncheon groups or other large gatherings, I would use these methods

Figure 15.2.   Materials used in "Weak in Body, Strong in Spirit: The Women's Suffrage Movement and Spiritualism" *Spiritualist Shorts* presentation, given to the Woman's Club of Erie, PA, 2018.
Image by Amanda Shepp.

in addition to bringing collection materials. I would circulate the facsimiles throughout the group during the "show and tell" portion and have the collection materials at a separate table nearby so they could be appreciated by attendees either before or after the presentation was finished.

*Spiritualist Shorts* mattered to the people who attended because these discussions provided a chance to take a close look at a specific facet of Spiritualist and Occult history. In a place where most people go to communicate with the dead or analyze their past lives, history has a very deep meaning to the community. Many visitors to Lily Dale are deeply interested in the past, especially when it provides a chance to better understand their belief systems or their own personal histories. From a special collections library standpoint, this program matters because it provides a unique opportunity to connect library patrons and history fans with rare books, archival ephemera, and interesting collections materials that are often seen as off-limits to those who are not serious academics. These "show and tell" type talks give a chance to put historical artifacts in the hands of people who normally wouldn't see themselves as important enough or deserving of such an intimate exposure to historical artifacts, and thus makes special collections more accessible and sometimes more interesting, but no less "special." Special libraries are full of history, even if visitors weren't expecting to find it there.

As with all of the programs at the Marion H. Skidmore Library, the *Spiritualist Shorts* ended with a prompt to take a program assessment survey or a patron survey. Often the responses to these surveys would lead to suggestions for future lecture topics. "Would love to learn more about mediumship history" or "Lily Dale history." Sometimes a patron would be fascinated with a particular book or author and put in a request for a deeper dive to be taken in order to gain a better understanding. "[Sir Arthur] Conan Doyle's Spiritualist beliefs and scientific research of Spiritualist phenomena would make an interesting lecture." Requests such as these always got a second look, as they were often niche and interesting subjects—a long-forgotten form of divination, like "GEOMANCY"; an author who wrote only one or two books during their very long career in Spiritualism, "Clara Barnett, please!"; or a misunderstood piece of Spiritualist history like "Houdini's visits to Lily Dale to bust fake mediums."

The reactions of audience members were also a good indication of the success of this program. Many program attendees would stay after (and sometimes well past closing time!) and engage in a further discussion about the lecture topic, take a longer look at the "show and tell" materials from our collections, or ask questions about what else I had uncovered in my research to prepare for the week's talk. Quite a few times, attendees would make an appointment to come take a deeper look at the materials used during the *Short* for themselves the following day. Their level of engagement with Spiritualist and Occult history, which was often their own communal history and was frequently spliced with a strong emotional charge to preserve and learn about that history, was very apparent. At the end of each summer season, it was clear these weekly short-format talks took figures and topics that patrons and community members had a minimal awareness of and turned that awareness into a full-blown curiosity, which in turn fueled a deeper passion to learn more about the roots of their individual beliefs.

To me, the true sign the *Spiritualist Shorts* lecture series was objectively successful was the number of repeat patrons it generated, along with the notable increase in summer foot traffic. Every summer, I would see familiar faces coming in each Tuesday for the weekly talk, and each year I noticed many of the participants staying in Lily Dale for longer stretches of time, or making several return trips throughout the summer season. Beginning just after the winter holidays, I would get visitors stopping in to ask what topics would be on the *Spiritualist Shorts* menu for the upcoming season, and interested patrons would often pass the news along to their potentially interested friends, whom I would inevitably see in the library that summer. To many of the septuagenarian patrons, these *Shorts* were a throwback to the workshops and lectures of the Lily Dale they first visited, a place where intellectuals could gather with like-minded people to learn about almost-forgotten moments in their history and celebrate these unique people, inventions, and creations. *Spiritualist Shorts* was a success because it sparked community interest in the library's collections for new generations of Lily Dale Assembly visitors, residents, and scholars in Spiritualism.

Before I started the *Spiritualist Shorts* series, the main attraction that the Marion H. Skidmore Library boasted was a daily film documentary about the history of Lily Dale, aired each morning for summer visitors in its classroom. Generally, visitors would bustle in and make a beeline for the classroom space, sit quietly for the duration of the video, and immediately stampede toward the exit, never to set foot in the library again nor to linger and experience its beautiful rare books and highly unusual collections. *Spiritualist Shorts* allowed new life to be breathed into the Marion H. Skidmore Library, encouraged people to see its contents as something amazing that contained the secrets of the past (and possibly the afterlife), and fostered a desire in the Lily Dale visitor community to get better acquainted with their local library and cultural history.

*Chapter Sixteen*

# Tracing the Past for the Present and Future

## *An Artist-in-Residence Program*

### Nancy Spector

Artists and historians are not all that different. For the artist, the remnants of the past can give way to new interpretations, imbued with emotion and made important by personal choice through the selection of which elements to combine, how to layer, what colors to use, and the decision whether to consider the impact of these choices on the viewer. A historian has to make the same decisions, although through a different lens, with different tools, and from a different perspective. It is from this lens a new artist-in-residence program emerged at the Albright-Knox Art Gallery.

The Albright-Knox Art Gallery (AKAG) is the sixth-oldest public art institution in the United States. It was founded in December 1862 as the Buffalo Fine Arts Academy and has over a 150-year tradition of collecting and exhibiting the art of its time. The over 6,000-piece collection includes works by artists from all over the world, including Claude Monet, Vincent Van Gogh, Frida Kahlo, Jackson Pollock, Georgia O'Keeffe, Pablo Picasso, Andy Warhol, and many others.

As a museum educator, there is nothing more exciting than your supervisor, the Curator of Education at a major museum of modern and contemporary art such as the Albright-Knox Art Gallery, mentioning the administration is thinking of starting an artist residency tradition and she wants you to research what other museums have done. An artist residency program is one in which artists are invited to a location away from their usual environment and obligations in order to provide time for reflection, research, presentation, and/or production. In our case, we wanted to find an artist to create artwork connecting our community to both current trends in contemporary art and our region's history and culture. I was hoping if the project came to fruition, I would be chosen as the Project Director. Many times, I had researched exciting ideas for the museum that were never embarked upon, but luckily this time, things were different.

Two years later in 2005, with our overall budget range determined, the museum began the selection process for its first artist-in-residency program. I was given the names of a few artists to meet with and did so when they visited AKAG to install their work during a major internationally recognized exhibition called *Extreme Abstraction*. These were artists the museum was interested in obtaining work from sometime in the future. This was very smart as it reduced our time and costs associated with interviewing artists, visiting studios, and asking for and reviewing proposals. I was looking to select an artist whose work I admired but also one with whom I personally clicked. I knew that during the intense period where we would work with each other, we would need that feeling of connection to best guide the project.

We decided our first artist-in-residence should be Ingrid Calame, an internationally known Los Angeles–based artist who traces in pencil the marks and stains found on streets, sidewalks, and floors that she transports in one-to-one scale tracings, re-layers and colors in her studio, and then turns into her drawings and paintings. The resulting traced marks are silent remnants of the past that, as Calame has stated, have "stopped short of being symbols—they are captured images that combine history, physical fact, decay, memory, and personal experience."[1] Calame had already been invited to residencies where she traced tire marks at the Indianapolis Speedway and the floor of the New York Stock Exchange, creating large abstract-looking paintings and drawings.

The Albright-Knox Art Gallery's connection to the industrial history of Buffalo and specifically the steel industry has many entry points. One of those is John J. Albright (1848–1931), whose wealth was generated by the railroad, electricity, and steel industries. He was the founder of the Lackawanna Steel Company that was eventually acquired by Bethlehem Steel in 1922. In 1900, during his tenure on the Board of Directors, Albright gave $350,000 to pave the way for the acquisition of the land to build the museum's 1905 Greek Revival–style building on Elmwood Avenue in Buffalo, New York. Albright hired the famous American architect E. B. Green to design this majestic landmark. The new building was planned to be completed for the 1901 Pan-American Exposition to house the major art exhibitions of this world's fair, but setbacks in obtaining the Italian marble used in construction delayed its opening until 1905.

Ingrid Calame was delighted to be selected as our first artist-in-residence. The partnership began with an overall introduction to Buffalo's rich history, with a focus on the twentieth-century industrial history. We shared resources and websites with Calame that focused on this specific aspect of Buffalo's past. From this source material, she noted places she thought would be interesting to explore for the kinds of marks she likes to trace during her September 2007 scouting visit. During that week, we escorted her to the Peace Bridge, the Rainbow Bridge, the ArcelorMittal steel plant in Lackawanna, the Robert Moses Niagara Hydroelectric Power Station, many abandoned or privately owned grain elevators along the Buffalo River, playgrounds, and any other sites we passed where she expressed an interest to visit.

After the weeklong visit, she returned to her studio in Los Angeles to propose the details of a three-week stay in June 2008, where she would live in Buffalo while producing the tracings needed as the raw material for her art. She selected four major tracing sites: the ArcelorMittal steel plant (formerly a part of Bethlehem Steel), several abandoned grain elevators that have since become Silo City (an art and performance site), an abandoned public wading pool at the Perry Projects in South Buffalo, and AKAG's parking lot.

Our education department's task was now to plan a series of events leading up to her visit, engaging as many people as we could in the Buffalo community and other educational institutions in her creative process, culminating in an exhibition that would feature the final artworks she would create. All of this also had to fall within our budget and fulfill our department's mission: to help our community understand, interpret, appreciate, and participate in the artistic process of artists of our time. We had to work with our technology department to plan documentation of the project, our marketing and public relations department to plan a website presence and other promotional products, our legal team to draw up contracts and agreements, and our curatorial staff to determine an exhibition size and dates, including shipping the final work (the size and nature of which was again as yet undetermined) created in her Los Angeles studio to the museum.

Calame's budget included buying thousands of feet of Mylar, her tracing material of choice, which is very expensive. Additionally, she requested knee pads, pencils, erasers, and tape. Payroll included twelve local tracers and an assistant she brought with her from Los Angeles whose job was to organize the tracing days and pack the drawings to be shipped back to Los Angeles where they could be unrolled and spliced together into four giant drawings—one the size of a wading pool, one the size of the production floor of a steel plant, one the size of our parking lot, and one a combination of smaller drawings from the walls of an abandoned grain elevator from which Calame would create her final work. Additional expenses included lodging, meals, and airfare for both Calame and her assistant, along with estimated shipping costs for the drawings and final works.

As with any fledgling project, negotiating a feasible budget is a daunting, yet necessary, component of a project plan. Our preliminary budgets were far apart. To find the additional monies needed for Calame's suggested project budget, we applied for many grants but we knew we needed to get at least one very large one for this project to move forward. Any museum employee knows grant writing is part of the story, and at any point along the way not raising enough money for a project can result in its cancellation. In conjunction with our development department, we applied for and were awarded a MetLife Museums and Community Connections Program grant for $50,000 in December 2007. We were fortunate to receive a few smaller grants also. Although these monies brought our budgets closer together, we were always mindful of the scale of this undertaking. Unexpected changes might occur as we proceeded.

In October of 2007, knowing that Calame would arrive in June of 2008, our education team began to brainstorm how to connect with the educational community we had built from running in-school and teacher programs, museum art classes, and free monthly community programs at the Albright-Knox Art Gallery. We wanted significant involvement in the artistic process from our community, so we selected two schools and an after-school program with which we had strong relationships to conduct workshops at their sites taught by their own employees and museum staff. We planned to offer similar workshops at AKAG in the same time period for our visitors.

From April through June 2008, we ran four workshops over a series of eight weeks at each of the schools and four Friday night workshops at the museum. During the workshops, students learned about aspects of Calame's art-making process and created artwork to be exhibited in the education department wing of the museum. These workshops focused on learning about mapping, blueprints, and positive and negative space. Participants made bird's-eye view drawings of their own homes, and traced places in their neighborhoods such as school basketball courts and gymnasium floors. They then traced those drawings onto Mylar, colored them, and layered them into beautiful abstract works of art with a firm basis in imagery from the real world. I, along with my education team, would teach one workshop every two weeks for each off-site class, and the next week their own art teacher would work with them to complete what they had learned about from us. We talked with the participants about the history of their homes and neighborhoods and asked them to imagine them inhabited by people who had lived there in the past in an effort to explain how Calame's process incorporates primary sources from history into an abstract visual art image. Essentially, we asked them, "What aspects of what you see and find in your home and neighborhoods are evidence of those who came before you?" We called our four free public workshops at the museum AIR (Artist-in-Residence) Calame 101 and held them during our monthly Free Fridays sponsored by M&T Bank. These workshops mirrored the content of the school and after-school workshops, each one featuring a different aspect of Calame's process. Later, when Calame was in Buffalo tracing, we scheduled each site to meet with her despite the tight schedule she was on.

In addition to working with schools, we partnered with Starlight Studios, a local artist studio created specifically for artists with special accessibility needs, to come up with a related project to exhibit their artists' work in the education department. They chose to look at the historic architecture of the Buffalo houses around their studio, many of which were built during Buffalo's industrial boom, but now sad reminders of the effects of the rust belt era. The artists walked the neighborhood, photographed and sketched the houses, and created wall hangings of materials of their own choice illustrating these houses.

Finally, we decided we wanted the voices of our community members whose lives had been touched by the steel industry itself. My education team and I identified community members and steel factory personnel to interview about their memories of living near or working at the steel plant now operated by ArcelorMittal Steel. One interviewee remembered her mother getting up to hang laundry in the middle of the night in order to avoid it getting covered in soot when the coke-burning ovens started shortly after sunrise. A steel plant worker remembered painting the very numbers Calame's team traced off the floor. Another recalled the camaraderie of the workers and how they watched out for one another during the long, demanding, and dangerous shifts, which he believed likely saved lives. The oral histories were sent to the museum's sound editor and resulted in clips of two minutes or less from each interviewee to accompany the exhibition in ways still undecided at the time of their creation.

The planning and implementation of this project involved meeting with many people from a variety of backgrounds. Calame's proposal included the hiring of a team of a dozen artist employees who would trace at the four selected sites during this three-week period, seven days a week, eight hours or more a day as necessary. The selection, management, and payroll for this team were among my responsibilities as project director. I interviewed and hired a team of local high school and college art majors, art educators, and emerging local artists whose names I saw grow in stature throughout their later careers in Buffalo and elsewhere. The selected team was convened the first day of the residency in June 2008 for a "practice draw" at the super-complicated surface of the chipping bright blue paint of the wading pool. They had to learn how to follow Calame's drawing instructions. She focused heavily on making complex decisions about positive and negative space in a drawing, an art concept that requires much practice to master. Only two older artists dropped out when they realized they might not be up to being on their

**Figure 16.1.** Artist Ingrid Calame directs the group how to carry out the initial tracing at an abandoned public wading pool at the Perry Projects in South Buffalo, New York. Courtesy of Ingrid Calame.

hands and knees for eight-hour stretches; luckily, we had hired a few more team members than we needed because we suspected this might happen.

Another group I planned and worked with was from ArcelorMittal Steel. I met with the production manager to work out the details for the tracings during the operational hours of the steel plant in June 2008. There were three, eight-hour shifts, seven days a week during which to make art. It had to be done when all the machinery and workers were operating as usual. Along with the production manager, I had to arrange a meeting to train the tracers about steel plant safety a few weeks before Calame arrived. Due to the very dangerous nature of the environment and despite the intense heat, it was mandatory for everyone to wear long-sleeve shirts, trousers, Kevlar protective sleeves, and steel-toed boots. All the tracers had to sign a release and agree to these conditions as safety was the first priority.

The final tracings during Calame's residency occurred during the M&T Bank Free Friday family night when it was planned she would complete tracings of AKAG's parking lot. Participants at the event were encouraged to trace their own sections of the parking lot in a special area. Calame and her team also were available to talk with museum visitors. Our photographer set up a time-lapse camera to document the parking lot drawing, and our security team oversaw the safety of all the visitors in the parking lot when the tracings were taking place. Parking accommodations were made at nearby State University of New York Buffalo State College since during this event much of the parking lot would not be available for visitors.

After her residency in June 2008, Calame decided she wanted to make a wall painting, a piece of art painted directly on the wall at the museum that is therefore deliberately temporary—it would be painted over for the next exhibition. She did not want just one wall, she wanted to use an entire room of the museum. This was not in the original plan, but after some negotiation with the curator, it was added because it fit the nature of the project so perfectly. Now part of the AKAG collection, the plans for this work are what the museum owns. Following these plans and with the materials to create them in storage, it can be re-created for other showings sometime in the future.

The final exhibition of *Ingrid Calame: Step on a Crack . . .* was on view at the Albright-Knox Art Gallery from September 25, 2009, through February 28, 2010. The exhibit consisted of two large galleries in the 1905 building of the museum. One housed the large wall painting, which was entirely composed of the numbers from the floors of the steel plant Calame and her team

**Figure 16.2. *Step on a Crack* . . . installation at the Albright-Knox Art Gallery, Buffalo, New York, 2010.**
Courtesy of Ingrid Calame.

traced in 2008 and replicated on the museum's walls. They were painted in silver color reminiscent of the steel that was produced at the tracing site. This exhibit room also included the oral histories of the community members and steel workers. These recordings were donated to the Steel Plant Museum of Western New York and are now a part of its permanent collection.

There were many successes and challenges from this artist-in-residence program. One of the major problems we encountered was the timing of the residency and follow-up exhibition. Had our team not compromised on the June 2008 residency date, maximum school participation would have been much easier to achieve if the visit had come earlier in the school year. Trying to coordinate programming, exhibitions, and personnel schedules was like fitting together pieces of a puzzle. Finding ways to get as many of the 250 students who participated in the site visit as possible to attend the exhibition was problematic due to the timing. Many students had new teachers, and some had even graduated from school. While Calame appreciated the extra time to create her final work, unfortunately many of the students never ended up seeing the finished exhibition.

It has been ten years now, and Calame's wall painting has long been painted over. The wading pool at the Perry Projects is now a splash pad; the AKAG's parking lot will disappear as the construction of a new building breaks ground this year; and ArcelorMittal closed their Buffalo plant not too long after the exhibition. The numbers on the floor might still be there today, but not for long. Not all of the students who were involved in the project were able to visit the exhibition, but the ones who did were beyond excited—they understood. In many ways, when they participated and created their own neighborhood tracings they had walked her walk—followed her process of capturing history itself in art. And now they may understand her talk—the way she visually communicates a narrative, like the history in and around a city, through her artwork.

## NOTE

1. *Ingrid Calame: Step on a Crack . . .* , Albright-Knox Art Gallery, accessed November 13, 2019, https://www.albrightknox.org/art/exhibitions/ingrid-calame -step-crack.

## Chapter Seventeen

# Getting You in the Holiday "Spirit"

## *It WAS a Wonderful Life!*

### Sandy Starks

Music, laughter, singing, and the bright lights of a theater in a cemetery? Yes . . . it's true. Founded in 1849, Forest Lawn is a cemetery located in Buffalo, New York. At the time, the original eighty acres were approximately two and a half miles outside the city limits. Forest Lawn was part of the rural cemetery movement that began in the early 1800s. Its concept became popular in the United States and Europe due to the overcrowding and health concerns of urban cemeteries. The cemetery was designed to be a landscaped, parklike setting with elaborate monuments, memorials, and mausoleums, many filled with Victorian symbolism and poetic verse. Charles E. Clarke, an attorney, may have had this idyllic vision when he purchased the picturesque area of rolling hills and meandering creek to become Forest Lawn. He had the land fashioned into an artistic but still natural setting where a family might wish to have a picnic close to their dear ones who had passed on. At the time, there was no public park to enjoy nature, so the cemetery became the place of relaxation. Today, Forest Lawn has expanded to 269 acres and is located in the heart of the City of Buffalo. It is now home to approximately 200,000 permanent residents with burials that still continue today. Forest Lawn is also at the core of western New York's cultural tourism renaissance. Each year, Forest Lawn hosts thousands of visitors who come to enjoy all it has to offer: sculptural masterpieces among unmatched natural beauty—hills, valleys, lakes, and streams. It is a site of living history. Most importantly, it contains the stories of those who now rest in peace under its care—from a US President and foreign royalty, to captains of industry, artists, inventors, veterans from every US conflict since the Revolutionary War and everyday people who quietly built the western New York community. Forest Lawn is listed on the State and National Registries of Historic Places.

In the center of the cemetery is a historic chapel in the Gothic Revival style that was originally built in 1881 with additions in 1933. In 2010, the chapel had just finished a complete renovation with the old stone masonry repointed, the roof repaired, the heating and plumbing system upgraded, the carved wood trim restored to its original luster, stained glass cleaned and repaired, the walls freshly painted, and the parking lot resurfaced. The intimate non-denomination chapel seats approximately seventy people in sixteen carved oak pews. Stack chairs are added to the space if a service or event is large. The small altar, historical Wurlitzer organ, rose medallion-like windows, and other stained glass windows give the guests a calming place to pray, meditate, or enjoy music, lectures, or other events. While the chapel was originally constructed for memorial services, with the renovation complete, a desire for further utilization of the building was considered.

In the summer of 2010, I met with the president of Forest Lawn and discussed plans about expanding our successful award-winning summer walking and trolley tour season into the late fall and winter months. The climate of Buffalo necessitates that winter programming be held indoors; therefore, we settled on a lecture series to show off the refurbished chapel. Many other cultural organizations transition to doing lecture presentations during the winter months, so we wanted to differentiate our offerings and be more innovative. Since we have a historic Wurlitzer organ in the chapel, we created a series of lectures that incorporated a musical component.

While this programming was successful, when it came to the month of December, we wanted to incorporate the spirit of the holiday season into our offerings. Who wants to go to a lecture during the pre-holiday weeks, especially on a Sunday afternoon? What do you do to create a tasteful program for this festive time? We knew there were many movers and shakers buried in Forest Lawn and that finding relevant material would be easy. We have access to more than 170,000 life stories, a restored historic chapel, and a reputation for creating fun, yet entertaining programs that teach about the people buried at the cemetery. We turned the chapel into a delightfully decorated theater, picked out stories from the "permanent residents" who are interred in the cemetery, created a musical play, and, voilà, a new program was born.

When I was explaining my concept for the program to Joseph Dispenza, President of Forest Lawn, he blurted out the title, "It WAS a wonderful life." Though we both were in a fit of laughter, we knew it was the perfect yet respectful twist to what is already a well-known holiday classic film—*It's a Wonderful Life*. It was a tongue-in-cheek concept for us to build on.

During the summer months on our Sunday ninety-minute trolley tours and walking tours, some of our permanent residents appear in period dress and tell our guests about their lives. Drawing on the success of these first-person narratives, we expanded on their life stories and included content about their memories of the holiday season. In order for this program to be successful, we drew on a number of partnerships and collaborations. I approached The Festival Chorus, a professional local choral group who had done many memorial programs for Forest Lawn, and asked if they would be interested in doing a holiday concert weaving in the appearance of our permanent residents during the performance. Their director was enthusiastic about this partnership opportunity. A Festival Chorus member, Ernie Churchill, created a story line that not only introduced the song selections but also tied the songs in with the biographies that were to be featured.

In the first production, The Festival Chorus, dressed in festive red, black, and white outfits, entered the chapel from a back room and paraded to a stage that was created in front of the altar that had risers and chairs. Once seated, there was a deliberate moment of silence making the audience wonder—what is going to happen next? From behind the audience, the first presenter, Mary Burnett Talbert (American orator, activist, suffragist, and reformer), entered singing a robust a cappella gospel version of the song "Mary Had a Baby," followed by her speaking about church activities and foods traditionally served in the African American community in the 1920s. Other actors portraying several permanent residents of Forest Lawn followed, each sharing their compelling story. John H. Dover, a sergeant who served in the Union Army during the Civil War as a member of the 54th Massachusetts Infantry, the first exclusively African American unit to fight in the war, spoke about the Christmas letters he sent to family members. George Norman Pierce, President of the Pierce-Arrow Motor Car Company, talked about the numerous events and programs that his many employees engaged in over the holidays during the turn of the twentieth century. In between each resident appearance and monologue, The Festival Chorus sang a joyful variety of holiday songs that included "Away in a Manger," "The Battle Hymn of the Republic," "Toyland," "It's Beginning to Look a Lot Like Christmas," "Silver Bells," "Jingle Bells," "The Christmas Song," "God Bless Everyone," and "Sleigh Ride." The concert ended with an upbeat version of Irving Berlin's "White Christmas," sung by Forest Lawn resident Dorothy Goetz Berlin, first wife of Irving Berlin who died shortly after they were married. The Festival Chorus joined in with a rousing finale. The production lasted approximately ninety minutes. After the first production of *It WAS a Wonderful Life*, we were inundated with phone calls demanding tickets, so we added another show the following weekend, which was sold out in a matter of hours.

Due to its popularity, the following year additional dates were added and a local director, Josie DiVencenzo, was hired to tighten up the performance and polish the staging. The tickets sold out in two days, and it was evident more shows were needed in upcoming years, which led to some logistical issues. Because the program takes place during the busy holiday season, it was difficult to get a large chorus to commit to multiple performances. We knew we had a winning idea, so we had to come up with a new plan.

It was decided after many brainstorming sessions to expand the cast of permanent residents and enlist the support of local theater and musical professionals. Joseph Demerly, a well-respected and talented actor who was then the Director of the Kavinoky Theatre, worked with Forest Lawn's Historian Patrick Kavanagh to redevelop our docent-training materials into scripts used in the production. Kavanagh was instrumental in getting information to Demerly about the people highlighted in the performance by finding any information about the individuals in Forest Lawn's extensive archives. Demerly himself did a lot of personal research via the Internet and local resources to develop the characters. In some instances, since information was vague there was a bit of "poetic license" that was used to tell a compelling, yet believable story. Additionally, Demerly hired a musical director, Michael Hake, who wrote the original title song and arranged the keyboard sections that became part of the program. Chris Cavanaugh, a professional lighting director, was brought in to build a stage, create festive mood lighting, and install a proper sound system.

For the seasonal production, the chapel and its exterior were decorated to create a warm and inviting atmosphere to present *It WAS a Wonderful Life*. Evergreen trees and wreaths, tasteful ornaments, poinsettias, and twinkle lights were purchased to adorn the walkway, reception room, and chapel interior. A lit gas fireplace added to the ambiance of the reception room. Warm red and green lighting in the chapel set the tone for the play while holiday music played softly as guests waited for the seventy-five-minute musical to begin.

New elements were added in this updated production. For example, in lieu of a large chorus singing the holiday songs interlaced with actors telling their stories, the cast who portrayed the permanent residents now also sang all the choral arrangements. Another change was the incorporation of Forest Lawn's history into the story line. In this new rendition, at the start of the musical play, John Lay Jr. and his entourage of permanent residents walk down the chapel aisle singing an original song written for the play, titled "It WAS a Wonderful Life." Mr. Lay was selected as the master of ceremonies because he was the first person interred at Forest Lawn in 1850. After he finishes his song, Mr. Lay introduces to the audience his "new family that resides on the 'other' side of the lawn" who then grace the stage.

Some of the same permanent residents and songs from the original production returned, such as Union Army Sergeant John H. Dover who sings "I

**Figure 17.1.  An actor portrays John H. Dover, who served in the Union Army during the Civil War.**
Courtesy of Forest Lawn.

Heard the Bells," Mary Burnett Talbert giving a powerful interpretation of "Mary, Did You Know?," and Dorothy Goetz Berlin ending the play with a high-spirited rendition of "White Christmas" with the cast inviting the audience to sing along.

New personalities were added. Robert B. Adam, owner of Adam, Meldrum and Anderson (AM&A) Department Store, speaks about the Christmas-themed window displays that the store was known for and about a little boy he encountered in the toy department looking for a gift for his mother. Adam sings the song "Old Toy Trains" to round out this scene. Al Boasberg—a well-known comedy writer from Buffalo who wrote for radio stars such as Jack Benny, George Burns, and Gracie Allen in the late 1930s—talks about the AM&A's windows and family Hanukkah celebrations . . . plus his untimely death! Another resident, Martha Tenny Williams, realized that children's needs were different from that of adults' when they were ill. Williams tells how she and her mother purchased a house on Bryant Street in Buffalo in 1892 and turned it into a hospital that specialized in the treatment of children. Today her legacy has grown into Buffalo's John R. Oishei Children's Hospital, one of the country's leading pediatric hospitals. "What Child Is This?" is sung after the telling of a story about a family who came to the hospital for help on Christmas Day.

Sir Frederick Cook has the funniest scene in the production. Dr. Frederick Albert Cook was an American explorer and physician best known for his claim of being the first man to reach the North Pole in 1908. His claim is

*Chapter Seventeen*

widely speculated to be false, and the discovery was later credited to Robert Peary who reached the North Pole in 1909. Cook's offbeat, quirky, and questionable tall tales revolve around his visit to the North Pole and an encounter he had with Santa Claus himself. A comedic rendition of "Jolly Old St. Nicholas" ends his scene as his friends on stage roll their eyes at his stories and antics.

One other addition to the production was permanent resident Marian de Forest. At the turn of the twentieth century, she was a journalist, playwright, and very active in the progressive women's movement. As the Founder of Zonta International and employed as a news editor, de Forest speaks about her efforts to break through the glass ceiling in the business world and follow her dream of writing plays. Her powerful performance is a heartfelt rendition of "I'll Be Home for Christmas."

In the film *It's a Wonderful Life*, an important part of the story includes reference to an angel. "Every time a bell rings an angel gets his wings," declares George Bailey's young daughter, Zuzu. At the entrance to Forest Lawn, there is a large bell that came from the now-torn-down St. Joseph's New Cathedral. This bell is rung as a "welcome" for every person who is laid to rest at Forest Lawn. The above film quotation and bell theme are woven into the production as told by John Lay Jr. This then concludes the production with the ensemble playing handbells during their rendition of "Carol of the Bells." After the musical, each guest is given a bell necklace attached to a holiday card, and the chapel carillon chimes an upbeat tune as guests exit.

While there have been some staffing changes, the production's new format remains largely unchanged. The original director moved out of state and a new director was needed. Loraine O'Donnell, who had been playing the role of Marian de Forest, was hired as the replacement. Her subtle, powerful suggestions took the show to another level with clever, yet simple changes such as different entrances and music arrangements. Like Demerly, she, too, was well connected in the theater community and able to attract the same type of high-quality actors and singers to the production. She also became the creative force behind the costumes for all of the actors, emphasizing both era authenticity and stage presence. Both Demerly and O'Donnell deserve credit for keeping the show fresh and of high quality.

Over the years, characters have been added or changed in order to encourage repeat visitation. For instance, the addition of permanent resident Shirley Anita Chisholm, first African American US Congresswoman representing New York State in 1968. In 2015, President Obama posthumously awarded Chisholm the Presidential Congressional Medal of Honor, so it was fitting we brought her story to life. Her song is "Silent Night" as she had fondly remembered being sung by all when she celebrated Christmas Eve with friends and neighbors.

**Figure 17.2.    An actress portrays Mary Burnett Talbert, American orator, activist, suf-
fragist, and reformer.**
Courtesy of Forest Lawn.

*It WAS a Wonderful Life* now has two matinee performances every Sat-
urday and Sunday for about six weekends starting right after Thanksgiving
and ending New Year's weekend. Because the chapel is in the middle of the
cemetery and the roads have no guardrails or lights illuminating the winding
passages, evening performances are not possible. Each performance accom-
modates one hundred guests sitting in the chapel's pews and chairs. Since this
show is suitable for almost any age, many families consider this their must-do
every holiday season. We hear the show is also a highly recommended event
to attend for visiting out-of-town guests. Before each show, guests are treated
to a cup of hot cider, and a pop-up gift shop is available in the reception area
to do some last-minute holiday shopping.

*It WAS a Wonderful Life* has received many accolades from the media and
the numerous guests who cause the production to be sold out each year. In
2012, the production received three and a half out of four stars by *The Buffalo News*. In his review, Ben Siegel stated, "What sounds like a morose, potentially morbid display of friendly ghosts and black-and-white nostalgia, is
actually a delightfully salient little piece."[1] In 2013, *Buffalo Spree* magazine
awarded Forest Lawn the Best Unique Theater Space and said, "The eloquent
production exuded true holiday charm in an over-commercialized season."[2]

The most rewarding part of this experience has been seeing the many smiles on the faces of the guests as they leave the chapel, all expressing what a wonderful time they had and shocked that it was performed, in all places . . . a cemetery! One of my most touching comments was from a woman who approached me after the show and wanted to thank me. She came to this performance because a friend gave her a ticket as a gift. She said her husband had been gone for three years and she dreaded the holidays since his passing. But for the first time since his death, she said this performance lifted her spirits in such a way that it made her realize she had a wonderful life with him, was thankful for the time she had with him, and had a good and prosperous life presently.

My initial goal of creating an entertaining, yet poignant production that showcases the lives of some of the people buried at Forest Lawn has been met. But what I found surprising, and has transpired, is an opportunity to make our guests realize that every life story is important and that everyone has a story to tell. It has put me on a quest to urge people to write their stories for future generations so their descendants know their family members did have a "wonderful life."

## NOTES

1. Benjamin Siegel, Review of "It WAS a Wonderful Life," *The Buffalo News*, December 12, 2012.

2. "2013 Best of WNY Winners," *Buffalo Spree*, accessed November 13, 2019, http://www.buffalospree.com/Buffalo-Spree/July-2013/Buffalo-Sprees-2013-Best -of-WNY-Winners/.

*Chapter Eighteen*

# All Are Welcome

## *The Museum as a Stage for Community Dialogue*

### Tara L. Walker

The Buffalo History Museum, originally the Buffalo Historical Society, was founded in 1862. With a collection of more than 100,000 artifacts, the museum cares for objects and stories representing the people and history of western New York, including information on the Haudenosaunee Native Americans, War of 1812, and the Erie Canal, as well as immigration, industrialization, and aviation eras. The current museum structure was built to be the New York State Building for the 1901 Pan-American Exposition and is modeled after the Parthenon in Athens, Greece. The Buffalo History Museum's Resource Center is about one mile southwest of the main museum and houses the 3,000-square-foot *Spirit of the City* exhibit, which showcases the story of the 1901 World's Fair and its most unique artifact: the gun used to assassinate President William McKinley.

Oftentimes, the large templelike structures of older museums, like the Buffalo History Museum with its columned entrance and marble steps, can be imposing edifices and a physical barrier to what lies within. While new community members may be eager to learn the history of their new home, they may not feel comfortable accessing it. Providing welcoming and engaging programming in unexpected ways for new residents can help to break down this physical barrier and allow visitors the opportunity to experience museums as educational sanctuaries.

In 2009 as the Museum Educator, I created the *Museum Introduction Program* for newly arrived immigrant and refugee communities in western New York. The goal of the program was to utilize the museum's artifact collections to help twenty-first-century arrivals learn about the history, art, and culture of Buffalo through guided exhibit tours and engaging hands-on activities that are English Language Learner (ELL) based. Museums and cultural institutions around the world are focusing more on how underserved populations are represented and engaged in programming, interpretive exhibitions, and artifact collections. International scholars and museum professionals are addressing both the difficulties and successes that many organizations face when discussing the histories of immigrants and refugees. Museums have an opportunity to serve as a stage for community dialogue, civic engagement, and social activism. Cultural institutions can strive to serve distinct populations with diverse members, individual stories, and particular needs.

There are distinct differences between immigration, internal migration, and refugee resettlement. An immigrant is a person who chooses to leave his or her country of origin to reside in another part of the world; oftentimes it is to seek better opportunities. In contrast, an illegal immigrant is an individual who enters a foreign nation unlawfully and resides in the country without sanction. Internal migration is the movement of people within a geographic area in which they have citizenship. Immigrants, illegal immigrants, and internal migrants are drastically different from refugees. Refugees are individuals who are forced to leave their homelands because of war, political oppression, violence, famine, religious persecution, or other life-threatening situations.

Between 2010 and 2014, the Census Bureau indicates 12,196 individuals from foreign nations relocated to Erie County in New York State.[1] These numbers are not unique to Buffalo, and museum programs like this can welcome all groups to a community and make history accessible. Individuals living in Buffalo are arriving from Burma, Bhutan, Nepal, Iran, Iraq, Somalia, Eritrea, Sudan, Rwanda, the Democratic Republic of Congo, Liberia, Russia, Cuba, Mexico, and Columbia. International refugees, immigrants, and internal migrants come from diverse backgrounds and cultures. Each ethnic group and individual case has a variety of needs. How, then, can museums and cultural institutions add another layer of service for these populations? There are four major social service organizations in Buffalo that assist new arrivals. These agencies provide services such as language and cultural orientation, food assistance, medical care, clothing, and employment training. Some individuals arrive with knowledge of the English language and experience living in urban areas. They will need only initial support with housing, registration for school, and job placement assistance. Others arrive without any English fluency and are accustomed only to rural settings. Once an immigrant or refugee is granted entry into the United States, they must complete interviews with the State Department, US Citizenship and Immigration Services, and Homeland Security. All refugees and immigrants are medically screened by a government-appointed health care professional and must undergo security clearance procedures.

Inspired by the needs of this growing diverse community, the Buffalo History Museum, along with the help of leaders in the refugee communities and ELL instructors, created the *Museum Introduction Program* specifically for immigrants, refugees, and migrant citizens. Participants ranging from children to adults experience guided tours that are designed for English Language Learners. Not only are these programs offered to encourage new residents to learn their community's history, they are also opportunities to meet new people, gain exposure to the English language, and feel welcome in a place built on community stories. Tours take place during the regular daily museum operating hours, typically twice a month. Each tour is booked on an individual basis. The museum's education staff works directly with the ELL instructor or a Buffalo Public School teacher to choose a tour date, time, and the exhibits to explore. The customizable program aims to help international community members learn about their new home in western New York and its rich immigration history.

The main objective of the *Museum Introduction Program* is to introduce refugee/immigrant participants to the history museum using engaging, hands-on activities. This includes both pre-visit and on-site materials for both youth and adult English Language Learner visitors. During the pre-visit portion of the program, the main goal is for each visitor to have some exposure to the program content before the scheduled trip to the history museum. ELL or Buffalo Public School teachers work with their respective populations to help acquaint them with how museums can aid in acclimating them to their new home. The teachers assist them in defining what a museum is and its purpose. They acquaint the participants with the various types of museums in western New York. Many ELL instructors and Buffalo Public School teachers use the museum experience as an extension of the English language instruction and include the terms shared in the program such as *artifact* and *exhibit* as vocabulary words in the classroom.

Because many community agencies and resettlement organizations have limited funding and resources for field trips, free admission is offered to all tour groups that schedule the *Museum Introduction Program*. Allowing underserved populations to visit at no cost eliminates any economic burden on both the resettlement organization and visitor. Traveling to the museum can also be connected to the ELL classroom curriculum as both youth and adult students must learn how to use public transit in Buffalo. The central location of the museum allows ELL instructors to create a lesson about using the public bus system when planning a visit.

For the on-site visit, the museum staff and docents reinforce the pre-visit goals. They ask the ELL visitors about what the roles of a museum are, what different types of museums are in the area, and what the definitions are for common museum terms. Because many visitors from these populations may have limited, if any, experience in a museum environment, the *Museum Introduction Program* clarifies the etiquette for visitors. They learn why not to touch artifacts or use flash photography, both of which are important rules for the safety of the collection. After the initial orientation to the history museum, the docent models "how" to visit the museum by exploring the interpretive exhibits and observing artifacts on display. Video, audio, and imagery are used to nonverbally communicate with immigrant and refugee visitors, although each tour is given fully in English. The museum tour is used as an extension of the English language classes offered by the Buffalo Public School system or the local resettlement agencies. The strong, meaningful relationships with the resettlement agencies, community leaders, and ELL Buffalo Public School instructors proved to be vital to the success of the program.

On the history museum tour, one of the exhibits that has held the most appeal for visitors is the Pioneer Gallery, which displays authentic artifacts from nineteenth-century Buffalo and interprets life about the Niagara frontier. One area of the exhibit includes a spinning wheel that is used to spin fiber into yarn and a loom, a device for making fabric from thread or yarn. Visitors from Nepal, Burma, and Bhutan connect to these tools and Buffalo's preindustrial beginnings because weaving is a large part of their culture. Ceremonial garments and secular clothes are made in these countries from machines that are considered older technology in the United States. One success of the *Museum Introduction Program* has been these unplanned connections and the Nepali, Burmese, and Bhutanese visitors' enthusiasm for finding how their native country's traditions link to the history of Buffalo. Visiting the history museum allowed twenty-first-century arrivals to have a unique experience in a safe learning environment and gave them an opportunity to become more accustomed to their new community.

The *Museum Introduction Program* can be customized depending on the group's needs. Other museum offerings are also modified to support this program; for example, the Immigration History in Western New York Tour has been given in conjunction with the introduction program. Along with the basic *Museum Introduction Program*, visitors also tour the Native American Gallery and the *Neighbors* exhibit, whereby they learn about the earliest inhabitants of western New York and the waves of settlers and immigrants to the area since the eighteenth century. They learn about local settlement patterns, immigrant experiences, and cultural group clashes. Similarities and differences between various ethnic groups are discussed as well. Ultimately, the visitors learn how their arrival connects to the history of immigration of western New York.

Because of the powerful partnerships developed through the *Museum Introduction Program* and its success, the history museum has looked for ad-

**Figure 18.1.** Exhibition, *Buffalo: Through Their Eyes,* at the Buffalo History Museum. Image by Tara L. Walker.

ditional avenues to empower the members of these underserved communities of Buffalo. One example is the 2011 temporary photography exhibition titled *Buffalo: Through Their Eyes.* This was a collaborative project with Journey's End Refugee Services and CEPA Gallery in Buffalo. The exhibit included photographs taken by newly arrived refugee artists from countries including Burma, the Democratic Republic of Congo, and Bhutan. Journey's End encouraged their clients and families to participate in the project, and CEPA Gallery provided disposable cameras and basic photography instruction classes to the participants. Twenty-eight refugees were asked to take photographs of anything around them including their new homes, neighborhoods, families, and places of employment. Several hundred photographs were developed, and in the spring of 2011 the Buffalo History Museum exhibited select works in their Community Gallery.

Another impact of the *Museum Introduction Program* and its community partnerships was the ability for the history museum to secure the donation of traditional garments from the Karen ethnicity of Burma. These handwoven cotton and silk garments made on the Burma-Thailand border were on display in the Community Gallery, a first for this group's material culture to be on view in this particular museum. The garments included a traditional head wrap called a Ko Boe and a wrap skirt called a Longi. Handmade Burmese bags and ceremonial shirts were exhibited as well. These textiles feature the Burmese dominant colors of red, white, and blue and buffalo horns, signifying strength and courage to the Karen people.

After its de-installation at the history museum, *Buffalo: Through Their Eyes* was also on temporary display in the E. H. Butler Library at the State University of New York Buffalo State College. From 2012 to 2013, the Karen garments were also featured in the history museum's 150th anniversary exhibit titled *Ever After*, which highlighted significant artifacts from the collection. Buffalo has always been a diverse city with culturally rich and varied ethnic communities, and one of the museum's responsibilities is to document, preserve, and share the stories of Buffalo's communities throughout time.

The *Museum Introduction Program* and its complementary exhibits and collection acquisitions demonstrate how museums can deeply benefit from developing long-lasting, meaningful relationships with community partners and immigrants, refugees, and migrant citizens. These few examples illustrate successful attempts at community engagement and relationship building. By respectfully representing twenty-first-century new arrivals in exhibitions, collections, and programs, and by including their creative work within museum galleries, museums can inspire their visitors to become more curious and involved citizens. Because of these visitor opportunities, community members learn more about their new neighbors and how international issues such as war, poverty, hunger, and discrimination can affect everyday lives.

Figure 18.2.   The Buffalo History Museum.

The purpose of this project was to create a community-based educational program about the cultural traditions and heritage of the western New York region. Museums around the world can help recognize the changing demographics of their communities and can engage with underserved populations to help tell and preserve their stories. Activities, programs, and exhibitions that engage underserved populations need to be engrained in every museum's mission, as these institutions are increasingly embracing the responsibility of serving as a stage for community dialogue and social awareness.

## NOTE

1. "City and Region: Immigrants End the Decline in Erie County Population," *The Buffalo News*, accessed April 23, 2015, http://www.buffalonews.com/city-region/eriecounty/immigrants-end-the-decline-in-erie-county-population-20150326.

# Bibliography

"2013 Best of WNY Winners." *Buffalo Spree.* Accessed November 13, 2019. http://www.buffalospree.com/Buffalo-Spree/July-2013/Buffalo-Sprees-2013-Best-of-WNY-Winners/.

Ackerman, Jennifer. Review of *The Extinct Birds Project,* by Alberto Rey, Fredonia, NY: Canadaway Press, 2018. Accessed November 15, 2019. http://www.extinctbirdsproject.com/book.html.

American Alliance of Museums. *Excellence and Equity: Education and the Public Dimension of Museums.* Washington, DC: American Alliance of Museums, 1992.

"Badges." Girl Scouts of Western New York. Accessed November 14, 2019. https://www.gswny.org/en/our-program/badges.html.

*Boston Daily Globe* Newspaper Archives (September 7, 1901), 4. Accessed May 5, 2019. https://newspaperarchive.com/boston-daily-globe-sep-07-1901-p-4/.

Buffalo Philharmonic Orchestra. "enLIGHTen Buffalo at the Richardson Olmsted Campus." Filmed July 28, 2017. YouTube video, 11:23, Posted February 13, 2018. https://www.youtube.com/watch?v=rVESXkC2rJs&t.

Buffalo Weather Bureau [National Weather Service] Records, 1878–1948. Library, Buffalo Museum of Science Research Library.

Calame, Ingrid. *Step on a Crack . . .* Albright-Knox Art Gallery. Accessed November 13, 2019. https://www.albrightknox.org/art/exhibitions/ingrid-calame-step-crack.

Child, Lydia. *The American Frugal Housewife.* Boston: Carter, Hendee, and Co., 1833.

"City and Region: Immigrants End the Decline in Erie County Population." *The Buffalo News.* Accessed April 23, 2015. http://www.buffalonews.com/city-region/eriecounty/immigrants-end-the-decline-in-erie-county-population-20150326.

Cole, Johnnetta Betsch, and Laura L. Lott, eds. *Diversity, Equity, Accessibility, and Inclusion in Museums.* New York: Rowman & Littlefield, 2019.

Curran, Pearl (Mrs. John S.), and Patience Worth (Spirit). *The Sorry Tale: A Story of the Time of Christ.* New York: Henry Holt and Company, 1917.

Dimock, Michael. "Defining Generations: Where Millennials End and Generation Z Begins." Pew Research Center. January 17, 2019. Accessed May 12, 2019. https://www.pewresearch.org/fact-tank/2019/01/17/where-millennials-end-and -generation-z-begins/.

Duncan, Alastair. *Tiffany Windows*. New York: Simon, 1980.

Everett, J. *A book for skeptics: being communications from angels, written with their own hands : also, oral communications, spoken by angels through a trumpet and written down as they were delivered in the presence of many witnesses: also, a representation and explanation of the celestial spheres, as given by the spirits at J. Koons' spirit room, in Dover, Athens County, Ohio.* Columbus: Osgood & Blake, 1853.

"Facilitated Dialogue." International Coalition of Sites of Conscience. Accessed July 10, 2019. https://www.sitesofconscience.org/wp-content/uploads/2019/01/ Dialogue-Overview.pdf.

Falk, John H., and Lynn D. Dierking. *Lessons without Limit: How Free-Choice Learning Is Transforming Education.* New York: AltaMira Press, 2002.

———. *The Museum Experience.* Washington, DC: Whalesback Books, 1992.

Fletcher, Anna Louise. *Between the Slates.* Washington, DC: Anna Louise Fletcher, 1934.

"Girl Scouts Carry on Belva's Legacy." Middleport, New York. August 14, 2017. Accessed November 14, 2019. http://middleport-newyork.com/girl-scouts-carry -belvas-legacy/.

"Guidelines for WNY Belva Lockwood Badge." Girl Scouts of Western New York (original 1986; revised 2011). Accessed November 14, 2019. https://www.gswny .org/content/dam/girlscouts-gswny/documents/co-Belva_Lockwood.pdf.

Hatrak, Amy, Frances Mills, Elizabeth Shull, and Sally Williams, comps. *Fanny Pierson Crane: Her Receipts, 1796.* Montclair, NJ: Montclair Historical Society, 1974.

Hofer, Margaret K. *The Games We Played: The Golden Age of Board and Table Games.* New York: Princeton Architectural Press, 2003.

Hoffmann, Donald. *Frank Lloyd Wright: Architecture and Nature.* New York: Dover, 1986.

Hubbard, Elbert. "A Message to Garcia." *The Philistine.* East Aurora, NY: The Roycrofters, 1899.

International Coalition of Sites of Conscience. Accessed July 10, 2019. https://www .sitesofconscience.org/en/home/.

Jackson-Forsberg, Eric, ed. *Frank Lloyd Wright: Art Glass of the Martin House Complex.* Petaluma, CA: Pomegranate, 2009.

Johnson, Paul. *Literacy through the Book Arts.* Portsmouth, NH: Heinemann, 1993.

"Juliette Gordon Low." Girl Scouts. Accessed November 14, 2019. https://www .girlscouts.org/en/about-girl-scouts/our-history/juliette-gordon-low.html.

Lamb, Frederick S. "The Making of a Modern Stained Glass Window: Its History and Process, and a Word about Mosaics." *The Craftsman* X, no.1 (April 1906).

Letson, Elizabeth Jane. *Diary.* Manuscript on file, Buffalo Museum of Science Research Library, 1901.

"Lumenocity." Cincinnati USA Regional Tourism Network. Accessed May 13, 2019. https://cincinnatiusa.com/events/lumenocity.

"McKinley Assassination Ink: A Documentary History of William McKinley's Assassination." (n.d.). Accessed May 1, 2019. http://mckinleydeath.com/documents/govdocs/transcript.htm.

Nesline, Brian. Museum of disABILITY History *Newsletter*. Summer edition, 2014.

Niagara Falls Underground Railroad Heritage Center. *Brand Document*. Manuscript on file.

Norgren, Jill. *Belva Lockwood: The Woman Who Would Be President*. London: New York, 2008.

"Our Hershey's Happiness History." HERSHEY'S. Accessed May 15, 2019. https://www.hersheys.com/en_us/our-story/our-history.html.

Pene, Xavier. *Darkest Africa; Real African Life in a Real African Village*. Manuscript on file, Buffalo Museum of Science Research Library, 1901.

Penney, Thomas. Leon Czolgosz Trial Scrapbooks. The Buffalo History Museum Library and Archives, Mss. D2011-01.

Post, Isaac. *Voices from the Spirit World*. Rochester: Charles H. McDonell, 1852.

"Quick Facts: Niagara Falls City, New York," United States Census Bureau, accessed February 11, 2020, https://www.census.gov/quickfacts/niagarafallscitynewyork.

Quinan, Jack, ed. *Frank Lloyd Wright Windows of the Darwin D. Martin House*. Buffalo: Burchfield-Penney Art Center, 1999.

Rey, Alberto. *The Extinct Birds Project*. www.extinctbirdsproject.com.

Richmond, Cora L. V., and Benjamin Rush (Spirit). *Psychopathy, or Spirit Healing*. Rogers Park: William Richmond, 1890.

Roosevelt, Theodore. *Theodore Roosevelt: An Autobiography*. New York: Charles Scribner's Sons, 1923.

Schonfeld, Roger, and Mariet Westermann. *Art Museum Staff Demographic Survey*. The Andrew W. Mellon Foundation, 2015.

Seymour, Mina S., and Robert Burns (Spirit). *Pen Pictures*. Lily Dale: Mina S. Seymour, 1900.

Sharp, Marguerite. *The Cook's Book: Including Bubble & Squeak and Apple Slump: and Many More Good Old-Fashioned Recipes*. n.p., 1986.

Siegel, Benjamin. Review of "It WAS a Wonderful Life." *The Buffalo News*, December 12, 2012, Gusto Section.

Smith, Kevin. *Exhibition Script; Through a Clouded Mirror, Africa at the Pan-American Exposition, Buffalo 1901*. Manuscript on file, Buffalo Museum of Science Research Library, 2001.

Spiegel, Karen (Girl Scout Leader). Telephone interview with author, July 15, 2019.

Stubbs, Edna. Telephone interview with author, July 8, 2019.

Sturm, James L. *Stained Glass from Medieval Times to the Present: Treasures to Be Seen in New York*. New York: Dutton, 1982.

Tevi, John. *A Tour around the World and the Adventures of Dahomey Village [sic]*. Manuscript from the collection of Sonia Tevi-Benissan.

"Traditions." Girl Scouts. Accessed November 14, 2019. https://www.girlscouts.org/en/about-girl-scouts/traditions.html.

"Who We Are." Girl Scouts. Accessed November 14, 2019. https://www.girlscouts .org/en/about-girl-scouts/who-we-are.html.

Wilcox, Ansley, to Cornelia Coburn Rumsey Wilcox, September 5, 1879. Correspondence. Theodore Roosevelt Inaugural Site Foundation Collection, Buffalo, NY.

# Index

# About the Editors and Contributors

## ABOUT THE EDITORS

**Jill M. Gradwell** is Professor and Coordinator of Social Studies Education in the Department of History and Social Studies Education at State University of New York (SUNY) Buffalo State College. Her research centers on teaching, learning, and assessing history and has been featured in *Theory and Research in Social Education, Social Studies Research and Practice, Journal of Social Studies Research, The Social Studies, Research in Middle Level Education Online, Middle School Journal,* and *Middle Grades Research Journal,* and she is the co-editor of the book *Teaching History with Big Ideas: Cases of Ambitious Teachers.* Gradwell has secured grants through the US Department of Education and the National Endowment for the Humanities. Among other awards, she has been honored with the Middle States Council for the Social Studies Harry J. Carmen Award and SUNY Buffalo State's President's Award for Excellence in Research, Scholarship, and Creativity. In the local community, Gradwell has served on the Boards of Directors of the Roycroft Campus Corporation and the Holocaust Resource Center of Buffalo. She currently is a Research Associate for the Buffalo Museum of Science and a Society for the Prevention of Cruelty to Animals Paws for Love volunteer with her therapy dog Bailey helping to brighten up days for children, nursing home residents, and respite care guest visitors.

**Kathryn H. Leacock** has degrees in Anthropology and Library Science from the State University of New York (SUNY) at Buffalo. She joined the staff of the Buffalo Museum of Science in 2003. She began her museum career as the Curator of the Charles Rand Penney Collection, a private collection in western New York. Experience in the private sector in addition to public institutions provides Leacock with a well-rounded view of museums. She also served as the Interim Director of Museum Studies at SUNY Buffalo State College before returning to her true love of collections management. Leacock is currently the Director of Collections at the Buffalo Museum of Science and Lecturer of Museum Studies at Buffalo State College.

## ABOUT THE CONTRIBUTORS

**Christine Bacon** entered the field of public history working in historical interpretation at Kykuit: The Rockefeller Estate, Philipsburg Manor, and George Washington's Mount Vernon, before coming on board at the Niagara Falls National Heritage Area and the Niagara Falls Underground Railroad Heritage Center, where she helped create the nationally award-winning permanent exhibition *One More River to Cross*. Formerly an attorney, Bacon holds a law degree from Rutgers University School of Law and a master's degree from Niagara University. She is passionate about helping people understand how history continues to shape modern society.

**Daniel DiLandro** has been employed as the Head of Archives & Special Collections at State University of New York (SUNY) Buffalo State College for the past fourteen years and has worked in this and other academic and corporate archives for more than twenty-five years. He received his Bachelor of Arts in English and Anthropology as well as his Master of Library Science degrees from SUNY at Buffalo. He is certified through the Academy of Certified Archivists. His particular professional focus is on local history as state history, state history as national history, and national history as global history.

**Corey Fabian-Barrett** is currently the Director of External Affairs at the Western New York Women's Foundation. Her prior work as the Programs and Communications Manager at the Richardson Olmsted Campus included the one-of-a-kind *enLIGHTen*, presented with the Buffalo Philharmonic Orchestra in summer 2017. Previously, Fabian-Barrett worked at the Nantucket Historical Association, the Council for European Studies, and the Greenwich Village Society for Historic Preservation. She has a Bachelor of Arts in History and Archaeology from Smith College and her Master of Arts from University College London, as well as certifications in web development, museum studies, and nonprofit management.

**Kristen Gasser** was Director of Publications for Firsthand Learning, Inc. and continues to serve on the organization's Board of Directors. Now based in the United Kingdom, Gasser is currently a Training Consultant for Worthwhile Training, an organization that offers training, consultancy, and support for businesses.

**Michele Graves** is the Community Relations Consultant for the Center for Health and Social Research, State University of New York (SUNY) Buffalo State College and Exhibits and Education Coordinator for the Black Rock Historical Society. She serves on the regional committees and local boards of Neighborworks America and Forest District Civic Association. She is a consultant for the West Side Youth Development Coalition, SUNY Buffalo State College. Graves is retired as the Community Liaison from the Buffalo Police Department. She has authored publications for the Buffalo Police Department, SUNY Buffalo State College, US Justice Department, American Alliance of Museums, and Black Rock Historical Society.

**Amizetta Haj** is the Marketing & Visitor Engagement Manager of the Roycroft Campus. Haj oversees both the visitor center and museum, and serves as a spokesperson for the campus to the media and the community. She holds a Bachelor of Arts in History and Anthropology, and a Master of Arts in Museum Education & Visitor Experiences from State University of New York Buffalo State College. Growing up in East Aurora, New York, with a passion for history, Haj took a particular interest in the Roycroft Campus.

**Lenora Henson** is the Deputy Director and Curator at the Theodore Roosevelt Inaugural National Historic Site in Buffalo, New York. As a historian with more than twenty years of museum experience, Henson believes in the power of history to provide inspiration and insight that help us navigate the complexities of the contemporary world.

**Suzanne Jacobs** is the Education Director of the Hull Family Home & Farmstead. Jacobs is a retired administrator from the Lancaster Central School District. Her love for history, teaching children, and personal learning brought her together with the Hull Family Home & Farmstead.

**Jane Johnson** is the Director of Exhibitions & Marketing at the Roger Tory Peterson Institute of Natural History. A western New York native, Johnson has been overseeing exhibitions, marketing, and visitor experience at the institute since 2014. In addition to these roles, she works closely with the special collections, incorporating them into the institute's exhibitions, education, and public programming. Aside from her work at the institute, she volunteers locally as a member of the Salvation Army Advisory Board, Treasurer of the Chautauqua County Visitor's Bureau Board of Directors, and more.

**Twan Leenders** is the President of the Roger Tory Peterson Institute of Natural History. Leenders is a biologist from the Netherlands and is interested in animal ecology and conservation management. A former researcher at Yale University's Peabody Museum and other institutions, before coming to western New York, Leenders taught biology at Sacred Heart University in Fairfield, Connecticut, and went back into the "trenches" of hands-on conservation research and education while leading the Science and Conservation Office of the Connecticut Audubon Society.

**Ann Marie Linnabery** is the Assistant Director and Education Coordinator of the History Center of Niagara. Linnabery earned her Master of Arts in American History from State University of New York at Buffalo and over the past three decades has worked at museums in Buffalo, Lewiston, and Lockport, New York. She has developed and implemented programs for audiences of all ages and has written historical articles for local, state, and national publications.

**David Mack-Hardiman** is Associate Vice-President of People Inc. and directs the activities of the Museum of disABILITY History. He is the author of *The Magic Fire: The Story of Camp Cornplanter; Of Grave Importance: The Restoration of Institutional Cemeteries; Smokey Hollow: The Shoebox Coffin;* and co-author of *The Colony Chronicles.*

**Gina Miano** has been the Director of Education at the Martin House since 2013. Prior to her work in Buffalo, she held different education positions at the Orlando Museum of Art, Historical Association of Southern Florida in Miami, and the Nantucket Historical Association.

**Jean Neff** is a retired Education Curator of the Amherst Museum, now Buffalo Niagara Heritage Village. Neff first learned about historic cooking from classes taken at The Farmers Museum in Cooperstown, New York. For over fifty years of employment and volunteering, she has presented these programs at sites such as the Luke Swetland Homestead, Prouty-Chew House, Rose Hill Mansion, Tioga County Historical Society, and the Amherst Museum.

**Alan Nowicki** came to the Roycroft Campus in 2010 by way of Public Broadcasting Service and is its current Program Director. Nowicki is responsible for all classes and programming on the campus, including tours, workshops, lectures, art shows, film society, and book club. He has twelve years of experience working in educational programming, professional development, and community outreach. Nowicki has also been a teacher for more than twenty years, having taught in every grade level from pre-kindergarten through college, specializing in art and history.

**Elizabeth S. Peña** currently serves as Director of the Center for the Arts & Religion and Senior Lecturer in Art, Anthropology, and Museum Studies at the Graduate Theological Union in Berkeley, California. Before her current position, she was Curator of Anthropology at the Buffalo Museum of Science.

**Alberto Rey** is Distinguished Professor at State University of New York College at Fredonia in the Department of Visual Arts and New Media. He is also an artist, ceramicist; videographer; writer; Orvis-endorsed fly-fishing guide; and founder/director of a youth fly-fishing program, Children in the Stream/4H. His artwork is in the permanent collection of close to twenty museums, and he has had over 200 exhibitions. Rey has written and illustrated two books, *Complexities of Water: Bagmati River, Nepal* and the *Extinct Birds Project.*

**Amanda Shepp** currently serves as the Coordinator of Special Collections & Archives in the State University of New York College at Fredonia's Daniel A. Reed Library Special Collections & Archives Division. Before that, she served the Lily Dale Assembly as their first degree-holding librarian from 2014–2018, during which time she revitalized the Marion H. Skidmore Library, the largest library of Spiritualist materials in the world. She presents and writes on topics related to digitization and historical subjects within the realms of Freethought, Spiritualism, and the Occult. When she's not elbow-deep in materials from a bygone era, Shepp can be found home-brewing, experimenting in the kitchen, and enjoying life with her happy-go-lucky husband, Chris, and enormous Norwegian Forest Cat, Kujira.

**Nancy Spector** has been bringing the visual arts into people's lives and communities for more than twenty years in western New York, having spent eighteen years in museum education. In her teaching and art practice, she strives to make interdisciplinary connections to help bring people together, make them smile, and inspire them to save the world. She completed her undergraduate work at Cornell University, and additionally holds a Bachelor of Fine Arts from The School of the Art Institute of Chicago and a Master of Science in Science Education from State University of New York Buffalo

State College. Spector is currently teaching grades K–12 with New York State Teaching Certification in both Biology and Visual Art.

**Sandy Starks** is retired Interpretive Program Director of Forest Lawn, a cemetery in Buffalo, New York. Starks is a graduate of State University of New York Buffalo State College with degrees in Education and Public Relations. Her career includes positions in the hospitality and food industry, and Western New York Program Coordinator for Road Scholar, where she developed programs focusing on the American Arts and Crafts Movement at the Roycroft and Buffalo art and architecture. At Forest Lawn, Starks developed and facilitated programs and tours that highlight the history of Forest Lawn and the western New York region.

**Tara L. Walker** is the Curator of Education & Visitor Engagement at the Castellani Art Museum of Niagara University. She is also an adjunct faculty member in the Art History with Museum Studies program at Niagara University. She received a Master of Arts degree in Museum Studies and a Bachelor of Arts degree in Art History from the State University of New York Buffalo State College. Walker's past experience includes the Peggy Guggenheim Collection in Venice, Italy; La Biennale di Venezia in Venice, Italy; and the Adirondack Museum in Blue Mountain Lake, New York.